William James Stillman

The Old Rome and the New

And other studies

William James Stillman

The Old Rome and the New
And other studies

ISBN/EAN: 9783337384098

Printed in Europe, USA, Canada, Australia, Japan

Cover: Foto ©ninafisch / pixelio.de

More available books at **www.hansebooks.com**

The Old Rome and the New
AND
Other Studies

BY

W. J. STILLMAN

AUTHOR OF "ON THE TRACK OF ULYSSES," "EARLY ITALIAN PAINTERS," ETC.

LONDON
GRANT RICHARDS
9 HENRIETTA STREET, COVENT GARDEN
1897

To

Professor CHARLES ELIOT NORTON *of Harvard University, sole survivor of that luminous circle in which once shone Lowell, Longfellow, Emerson, Holmes, Agassiz, etc.—circle to whose intellectual hospitality I owe my imprimatur for American letters—this Volume is affectionately dedicated, in memory of our forty years of fraternal relation and sympathy.*

THE AUTHOR

PREFACE

The papers comprised in this volume have been printed in various magazines and reviews in England and America during the years between 1867 (My Experience in a Greek Quarantine) to 1895 (The Old Rome and the New), the only earlier paper being "The Subjective of It," the date of which I cannot recall, nearer than to say that it was one of the first contributions I made to the Atlantic, when Lowell was the Editor, and its articles were printed anonymously. They are selections from the wreckage of a life which has reached the limits beyond which it cannot be said that there is no hope, but at which reasonable men should be resigned if there should be none, and at which the highest good seems tranquillity, and the highest wisdom resignation. Of that life in its entirety, not uninteresting in adventure, and marked by some strange experiences in men and things, I hope shortly to tell the story. The most of what I have written during it is well lost, unsigned in pages of periodicals from which I have no desire to hunt it out. But the natural and harmless vanity of a man who has earned his bread by literature is to hope that something may survive him, which shall serve to keep him alive, at least in the memory of his descendants and

PREFACE

those of the friends who walked the same road with him, at the same time. And with this let us be content—few, indeed, are they whose writing survives their epoch, and in the multitudinous drift of humanity into oblivion, let us console ourselves that we are always in the enormous majority.

Beginning, as most young writers do, with more ambition than sound knowledge of my competence, I had the good fortune to learn soon that the opinions of young men are rarely worth preserving, though their art may be so, and I then decided that I would publish nothing before I should be forty: when I was forty I postponed to fifty: at fifty I said, sixty is not too late: and at sixty I had still too much to learn and I would trust to seventy. And now, at seventy, I would fain wait a little longer, were eighty assured, feeling my incompetence more keenly than even at thirty. Partial infractions of such a resolution could not be avoided by a man who had only his pen in place of a fortune, but I can honestly say that of my own ambition I have sent out nothing between book-covers except from a sense of the obligation to make known things which I thought the world ought to know, like the history of the Cretan insurrection of 1866, and the heroic revolt of the Slavs of Herzegovina in 1876. But I have been true to my principles in that, though what I wrote in my immaturer state is now put forth in a book, I have revised and re-considered what I then wrote, and am prepared to stand or fall in the opinion of my critics by what is printed. Whatever there

PREFACE

is of narration in the following pages is fact, even to the curious experience recorded in "The Subjective of It," with the exception of an unimportant detail in the Quarantine story, which as a whole is a re-arrangement of actual incidents, but drawn from two distinct experiences; but where they are the expression of opinions I hold them with a deference for that collective wisdom which finally prevails over all error. I belong to my epoch and do not pretend to be wiser than it; and if in relation to Art I hold my opinions strongly, it is because I have done my best during fifty years to fit myself by the study of all early and great Art to form them. If in the two Art studies there are repetitions, this was hardly to be avoided in two papers written with a long interval for different periodicals on the same theme. The same idea appears in different relations, and to condense the two into a single article I found impossible. Let me hope that repetitio juvat.

Milford, Surrey, 1897.

CONTENTS

	PAGE
THE OLD ROME AND THE NEW	1
MARATHON AND ITS BRIGANDS	25
MY EXPERIENCE IN A GREEK QUARANTINE	40
AN AMERICAN'S REVERIE OVER LONDON	63
JOHN RUSKIN	92
A FEW OF LOWELL'S LETTERS	128
THE DECAY OF ART	168
THE REVIVAL OF ART	198
THE SUBJECTIVE OF IT	232
THE PHILOSOPHERS' CAMP	265

THE OLD ROME AND THE NEW

THERE is something in the fascination of Rome that escapes my power of analysis. A generation has passed, and a second is on its way, since I first came under its witchery; everything is changed in it that can be changed in a city; what can be done to break the antique charm has been done, as if in malice—mutilation, renovation, desecration: and still it keeps the charm, like a masterpiece of Greek sculpture which has gone through the hands of barbarians, and come out shattered, maimed, and so defaced that only the eye of an artist can see what the artist meant by it. It is not its history nor its topography, neither its architecture nor its art, that makes it what it is: something of all these, perhaps, but beyond these something that defies definition—a kind of spiritual polarity which made it from the beginning the point to which turned whatever there was of aspiration in the Old World, and, long before the first wall was built on either Aventine or Palatine, determined its history fatally; and that, time after time, when an enemy had broken its strength and subjected its people, brought the remnant back to renew the struggle against time, and make the declaration of eternity, "*Urbs Eterna.*" It is not by many the oldest imperial site, and it has absorbed cities centuries older than itself, and which were probably such when the Ager Romanus was being formed by the eruptions of the Alban volcanoes. For Rome is built on some of the newest land on the earth, and Father Tiber once found the sea at the northern edge of the plain. The wandering tribes of Latin shepherds, who built their huts on the Aventine, probably came down from their Sabine hills as soon as the cinders turned to soil, and goats found browsing and sheep grazing; and ever since men have obeyed this unique attraction.

In Hellas humanity found the expression of the virtues and qualities, weak and strong, of its youth: art, poetry, the perception of the beautiful, the first maturing of philosophic intuition, the harmony and the inspiration of a happy, healthy, intellectual life, over which no shadow of oppression, spiritual or political, had come—the perfect perception of the beautiful and the ideal which is the visible form of the spiritually true; and with these defects of youth, that precocious humanity which was never to become manhood, but which would never again be rivalled as youth. In Rome humanity "came of age," as we say of the youth of twenty-one; judgment and power and common sense, the strong hand of empery, the fixed determination of him who has found his vocation,—namely, to rule the world,—came to it. Here the civic virtues set up their school; heroism of the sterner vein, law, which brought the sacrifice of the impulse to principle, and the individual to the state, and so evolved civilisation and empire. What the Greek was in his bloom-time he remains, less the virtues which belong to youth, plus the vices of decay. So the Roman ran through the flush of manhood to its decline; youth he never had, and a serene and sublime old age he did not reach, but the manhood was long and tenacious, dying finally by the vices of manhood as the Greek by the vices of youth, yet dying hard and late. It was as if the Roman character were exhaled from the soil, and possessed from birth a dogged vitality like that of some of the lower organisms, foreign to all ideal beyond that of the Civis Romanus; producing at no epoch the finer fruits of the human nature; borrowing its religion from Etruria, Greece, Egypt, Jerusalem, or Constantinople, its art from Athens or Tuscany; no great original artist* ever to this day coming to the surface from the depths of that state-incrusted existence. All that was finest the Roman had to borrow, but he borrowed it as he learned to use it. Only one thing Rome created for humanity as Greece had created art—the organisation of the *res publica* and law, which is its logarithm.

But why Rome should have fallen where it did is to me inexplicable. Climb the Capitol tower, and you see below you a group of insignificant

* With the sole exception, so far as I know, of Giovanni Costa, the living landscape painter, one of the type of Th. Rousseau, whom he resembles more than any other.

elevations in the midst of a wide plain, bounded on two sides by ranges of limestone hills, the nurseries of the Volscian, Hernican, Sabine, Umbrian, and Etruscan powers; and on the other two the plain melts into the sea, some fifteen miles away. It is neither a sea site nor a hill site, this group of little hillocks, which the ancients called their seven *montes* and we call the "seven hills." Nor, puzzling my brains for years, have I ever been able to understand why, from physical causes, Rome should have been Rome, and Athens only Athens. I used to think, when reading the Æneid at school, that Æneas was a fiction of Roman vanity, envious of the demigod founders of other states; but, divested of some of the purely mythological elements, the Trojan migration to Latium is shown, by the most recent archæological discoveries, to have some foundation in fact. To get at it, however, we must first understand that the Trojans were a race of the same stock as the Greeks, and that the feud which ended in a struggle that is known, or symbolised, as the siege of Troy, was really the first recorded of the rivalries by which the Greeks committed racial suicide, not a war between Asia and Europe. The more I study the evidences of authenticity in the ancient traditions, even those which are so mingled with theistic mythology that we have generally considered them as inexplicable fable, the more I am convinced that usually these traditions contain a solid basis of historical fact. Through the series relating to the Greek and Italian civilisations there runs a thread indicating an extremely early community, and that the movement began in Italy and went eastward to Asia Minor, returning later through Greece to Italy. Of this movement, known in all the early traditions as Pelasgic, the Greek and Trojan agglomerations were final and contemporary results. Amongst the traditions bearing directly on the Pelasgic origin of Troy is one recorded by Virgil, who says that Dardanus came from Italy. He is supposed to have gone from Cortona, which was the stronghold and latest refuge of the Pelasgi, so far as we know, and we have the tradition of the building of the first walls of Troy by Hercules and Neptune, who were distinctly Pelasgic gods, of the stock of Saturn, whose realm was Italy. The worship of Athena, the patroness of Troy, and the protection offered by Juno, the patroness of the Argives, the heirs and descendants of the wall-building Pelasgi in the Peloponnesus, a protection so warm as to cool her friendship for the Argives themselves, are further arguments for the identity of the races; and the subsequent migrations of Trojans and Greeks together to Italy and Sicily bring us almost to historical tradition. Segestæ was settled by a band of Greeks with a Trojan leader, and the earliest traditions of Trojan movements mention the presence of Greeks. Virgil represents the settlement in the Tiber region of Æneas and his clan, while we have the corresponding tradition that Falerii was founded by a colony from

Argos, who built there a copy of the great temple of Hera in the Argolid. The recent excavations on the site of that city show that, though for centuries considered Etruscan, and really included in the so-called Etruscan league against Rome, Falerii was never Etruscan, but for centuries preserved its Greek character, becoming Italicised only shortly before the period of the great Roman movement northward, not far from the time when Veii came under the rule of Rome.

The systematic excavations being made in the country about Rome have had for one surprising result, besides showing that the Greek individuality of Falerii was preserved till the Roman conquest, the indication that the influence of the Greek colonisation of that city, or something accompanying it, extended over the entire region, traces of the same arts being found at Antemnæ, Lanuvium, Alatri, and Veii. This does not apply to the ordinary art of Etruria, which was derived from the Greek, but took on a colour of Etruscan temperament in its development; for this Faliscan art is quite distinct in all its forms from anything Etruscan, and it maintains its type to the period just prior to the Roman dominion. The objects found in the Faliscan excavations, now in the new Roman museum of the Villa Julia, give us the history of that city from the earliest period of Italic civilisation to the destruction by the Romans. The first pages of this record tell the universal story of the Italic tribes from the shores of the Basilicata to the Apennines—a common civilisation extending back to an epoch of immense antiquity, which the students of it think they can carry back beyond fifteen centuries B.C. It is probable that this was a composite race in which the Siculi, the Umbri, and the Pelasgi were the principal elements, the last dominating until merged in the Italic. The distinctive Greek contributions in the stratification of the deposits begin not later than the eighth century B.C., Attic pottery being found in the tombs, but of an extremely archaic type; and the evidence grows stronger till the sixth century, when the ceramics are very largely of well-known Attic types, and, though always accompanied by home-made ware of a rude character, finally reach the highest attainment of Greek production. The tombs also give evidence of great riches and intimate commerce with Greece, vases being found bearing names of Attic painters. During the sixth and fifth centuries the Attic influence is supreme; with the fourth a change takes place, and the imported work appears no longer, but in its place a Faliscan art, which is in some cases of extreme beauty, though it is the beauty of the decline of art, which continues till the time of the destruction. The fragments of the statuary found in the temples are of a pure Greek art, and though of terra cotta they are as fine as anything of the fourth and third centuries discovered in Greece. The inscriptions which appear in the fourth century are in Latin, archaic but distinctly Latin, and one vase, which is an excellent copy of Greek work, bears the names of the Olympian deities in the Greek characters of the time, but in Latin—"Minerva" for "Athena," "Cupido" for "Eros," and "Zeus Pater" for "Zeus." The Latinisation has become complete. The beginning of this change, and the severance from Greece and the loss of Greek commerce must have taken place about a century before the time of the capture of Veii and Falerii by the Romans.

The slight researches in the Ager Veientinus have given similar objects; and as we know that the patroness of Veii was Juno, shown by the legend of the taking of the city and the removal of the image of that goddess to the Aventine, we may expect that in the future systematic excavations we shall find the same evidences of the affinity of that city with Falerii which we find both nearer and farther away. Thus, the revelations of archæology confirm the Virgilian tradition, and that other which states that before Rome there was an Hellenic influence imposed on the development of the Tiber valley, and that, under the hypothesis that the Trojan and Greek were of the same stock, it may literally be true that a Trojan chief led a band of emigrants to the Latin shores; but the tradition of the foundation of Alba Longa, like that of every other foundation by the Greek migrations, must be taken as meaning that the emigrants occupied a city already in existence, and apparently united with the former population. When the same kind of researches which have been so productive at Falerii shall have been carried out at Ardea, Lavinium, and Laurentum, localities particularly identified with the traditions of the Æneid, and at which no excavations have been made, we shall know more about the general character and local variations of the so-called Trojan migration; but we know already there is the highest probability that they were all under the same influences, and that the line of demarkation of the region so influenced was somewhat to the north of Falerii, beyond which the immigration imposing itself on the composite Italic element was Etruscan, no evidence of which is found in Falerii or in the Latin towns; and as on both sides of this line appears the evidence of the earlier uniform Italic civilisation, we have the right to assume that the Hellenic and Etruscan immigrations were so nearly coincident that the one locally excluded the other, and that they were both superposed on the Italic population, which here became Latin and in the north Etruscan. Of this so modified stock, the central point of gathering became Rome on the south and Clusium on the north.

From that time forward Rome has been the most powerful centre of attraction on the surface of the earth, first to the Old World, and later to the New. Even to-day, wreck as it is of its old glory, it is more peculiarly the "city of the soul" than any other that we visit. With due respect for the theories of others, this is to me unaccounted for by any evident reason; neither the republic, nor the empire, nor the church can explain it, but rather this mysterious attraction explains them. When I first came to Rome there was a curious phenomenon which struck me—the gathering together of peasants from the outlying villages on festal days, at certain localities where there was no visible attraction, neither wine shop nor lottery office, and not even an open place for the gathering, but a narrow street and a narrower sidewalk. One of these spots, which I was in the habit of passing, I found, by reference to the map of the ancient city, to be in the space once occupied by the forum of Nerva; and the only solution of the problem that appears to me is that, in a remote epoch, this had been the marketing place of the ancestors of these peasants, who, by the unintelligent, hereditary habit, always gathered there to hear the news and meet their gossips or clients. Rome was then full of such survivals of ancient customs, some of which continue, as may be seen in the Piazza Montanara, where the agricultural labourers still go in their picturesque costumes to make their engagements with the *padroni*.

In those days the Pope was king; life was cast in the mediæval mould; all progress was an offence, not only to the custom of the place, but to the fitness of it, and the new-comer had hardly ceased to be new when he became conservative and citizen of this imperial Lotophagitis. Existence was a dream, and almost as cheap as one; there was no morning paper to harry our serenity, or thrust the daily disaster of a distant and indifferent community on our tranquillity; we learned of most events when they had ceased to be startling. After the church, art was the theme of most thought, and the artist was the most important being after the priest. Roman life had its tides—high spring at Christmas and Easter, and dead ebb at midsummer—but there was never any bustle or fever of business; there was no growth; there were no new houses; there was no blocking the streets with building material, no laying of drains or disturbance of the soil, no enterprise, and no new trades. The head of the great hospital of St. Spirito was one of my friends, and in conjunction with him and two or three capitalists I organised a syndicate to supply the hospitals and city with American ice at the price, delivered at Civita Vecchia, of the snow, which was otherwise the only resource, delivered at the pits on the Alban hills, where it was stored for summer use. But the offer was refused; it would have disturbed the vested rights of the snow-harvesters. The sick in the hospitals had been so served for hundreds of years, and might be still. Every innovation was resisted as of the devil, and the possible horse of Troy for stealthy invasion. Rome had so maintained its position for the centuries of the papal rule; why change?

Outside this compact, grey, silent city, in which the picturesqueness of the *ensemble* was so in contradiction to the stiffness and general ugliness of the details, was a cordon of gardens and vineyards overlying ancient villa sites, abounding in the most interesting material; ruins in an almost infinite variety in their pathetic abandon to the dissolving influences of nature — baths, tombs, temples, theatres, palaces, aqueducts; and outside them, and the most picturesque of all, the old Aurelian wall, which meandered across highway and through villa grounds, a simulacrum of defence, but a most eloquent record of dead empire, marking the recession of its inhabited region; then, beyond the debatable ground between occupation and desolation, came the Campagna. The Campagna of Rome has become the commonplace of poet and orator when they have to deal with fallen grandeur, but no poet or orator, unless he were a painter, ever saw more than a fraction of its beauty; few even of the landscape painters have seen it all. There were, in those years of which I write, some who passed their lives in the hunt for its "subjects"; painting till the twilight came on; hurrying in to pass the gates before they closed for the night, reckless of the chill and the night-mists which even in midsummer follow the day, content to run the risks of malaria if so they might catch the intoxicating impressions of that unique and supreme nightfall, with its tremulous purple sky behind the purpler Alban hills at the east, and its mellow gold at the west, blinding the eyes more by the expanse of its glow than its brilliancy, more by the deep intensity of its light than by glare; by that luminous depth which is more the quality of the Italian atmosphere than the intensity of its blue, or the variety of colour on the sunset clouds. He who lived amidst these influences in the young enthusiasm of art and beautiful nature will remember the Campagna as he will remember no other landscape on earth; it is like a phrase of the noblest poetry, ineffaceable from its unapproachable simplicity. In those days, the joyous fraternity of the brush were to be seen on every road that led into the Campagna, at almost every season of the year. Down the Tiber, even within the city walls, pictures made to hand met the eye at every turn of the river; one found Claude and Turner wherever one went.

That phase of Rome is gone forever—gone as surely as the simplicity and stern morality of the republic, the splendour of the empire, or the moral oppression of the papal rule. Rome can no more be the home of art again than it can be the seat of universal empire or the patrimony of St. Peter. What has come is not so clear. The Romans of to-day have none of the distinctive virtues of either preceding epoch, except military courage, which the Italians have never lacked, though they have not always been fortunate in the employment of it. Taste was never a characteristic of Rome at any age, but in the great days the Romans built well. This cannot be said now, and all that is most modern is most execrable; all that is oldest is most execrated and profaned. The new barbarians who, in the present dispensation, swoop down from cisalpine Gaul, reared in the civic ideals of Genoa and Turin, have no sympathy with the monumental records of Rome, and no conception of anything to replace them. The Rome of 1870 was dirty, but dignified; inconvenient for people with modern tastes, but most comfortable for those who had adapted themselves to its mediæval ways. The Rome of 1897 is comfortable for nobody; the miles of new streets are filled mainly with huge, ugly tenement houses, stuccoed flimsies, abhorrent without and inhospitable within — a tasteless waste, where the highest virtue is fragility and the noblest destiny demolition. Of the delightful gardens which used to exist within the circuit of the wall of Aurelianus, the only considerable fragment remaining is that of the English Embassy; and that, too, had been marked out in building lots, and has been saved only by the protest of Her Majesty's Government backed by the *Times* and the Italian archæological authorities. The famous Ludovisi gardens, the pride of papal Rome, and amongst the most beautiful in Europe, have been built over, and the vengeful lover of Old Rome sees with a malignant satisfaction the long rows of untenanted windows of the huge apartment houses of the quarter, over whose portals, newest in stucco and whitewash, he reads the last remnant of the language of the Romans, "*Est locanda*." The Ludovisi gardens were offered to the municipality for 3,000,000 lire, and refused, while it spent 3,700,000 lire in the purchase and demolition of a single palace on the Corso, to make a vacant space less than the hundredth part of the gardens.

THE OLD ROME AND THE NEW

The transformation of Rome during the past twenty years is unique in the history of civilisation for barbarism, extravagance, and corruption; never since the world began was so much money spent to do so much evil.

But Rome survives it, as it has survived the wrecking of the Goths, the Vandals, the Constable de Bourbon; survives even the Barbari and the Barberini. The Campagna still undulates into distance, if somewhat encroached on near the walls, and the arches of the Claudian aqueduct still measure off the space with their gigantic stride; the Appian Way is not made a modern cemetery, and there is left material for the artist who has the courage to return; Aricia, Nemi, Tivoli, and the far-off Olevano remain unchanged. The papal city has been comparatively little altered by the expropriations except along the Tiber, and nobody need go to the new quarter who does not choose so to do. Life is dear, too dear for the cosmopolitan artist folk who used to make one of the principal attractions of the city to westerners, and with very few notable exceptions they are succeeded by modern Italians, of whose art little is to be said. There is old Giovanni Costa, like Titian, outliving the school of poetic landscape, and generously teaching its traditions to such as will learn them and the Academy of France, until lately presided over by the veteran Hébert, the last of the school of healthy religious thought in painting — that to which surfaces were not enough, and who were more troubled as to what they should paint than how they should paint it: but neither the one nor the other has had much influence on the younger men. The Café Greco, founded in the day of Salvator Rosa, has become a German pastry-cookery, and the place where once all the artists of Rome used to meet, along with poets and the minor brood of the Muses, is no longer to be recognised by the relic-hunter. Details disappear, but the eternal city looms above them like Mont Blanc over the little intervening hills when seen from a distance, or like St. Peter's from the Campagna, and will do so, when the present system is in ruins and ivy grows over the new quarter. All these crudities will disappear; this pinchbeck Paris is only another illusion which time will dissipate, and Rome will be again what it has always been from its republican days, even though the new republic comes and the papacy departs, a centre of attraction to a spiritual cosmopolitan population, never a centre of trade or business; and the people who know it are not those who are born in it, but those who are born to it and its liberties of thought.

In the cosmopolitan sense, it was a great misfortune that Rome became the capital of Italy, but it was fated. The same attraction that drew the Greek, the Sabine, the Gaul and the Carlovingian, the Etruscan Pontifex Maximus and St. Paul, has brought the Garibaldian and the house of Savoy. But, after all, the interference with the true enjoyment of Rome by its real citizen is not great or material. It will be a place of pilgrimage to the Catholic when the Pope has gone, if he ever goes; the historian, the archæologist, the poet, and the artist will always be its citizens, though holding no allegiance to Pope or King, subject neither to taxation nor conscription, and though disinterested in its real estate. He owns it who feels its spiritual (not ecclesiastical) attraction. To him there is no city on the earth which can content him after it. He may live in New York or London, Venice or Naples, but will always be more or less a stranger there, and be ready to go back to Rome. The new civilisation, while it has done much to disfigure and degrade the city, has also done much to improve it: made it cleaner and healthier, expelled the highway robbers from the streets and the brigands from the Campagna — matters of less importance to the true Roman than to the prosperous man of business, but to none indifferent. Life is dearer than it used to be, but the rate of insurance on it is lower and the ratio of the doctor's bill less, and the cost is not prohibitory to the man of small means. He who lives in his own house in Mayfair or Fifth Avenue is content in Rome with a small apartment in a crooked street, and on the third or fourth storey, and does not so stand on state but that he has his dinner in from the nearest cook-shop and his wine by the flask; has one servant, instead of three which he used to have when on his social dignity; uses cabs, and thinks it no derogation not to keep a carriage, and so lives on the rent

B

of his house in Mayfair. There are still quarters to be found in the old palaces in the papal city, but for people accustomed to fires there is sometimes a difficulty in keeping warm; for the Italians have a superstition about fires, and so it happens that instead of the cheerful grate one has to be content with a stove, whose pipe may go out at the window, in one or two of the chambers, and be dependent on the rarely absent sun for the rest. The fuel is dear, but then little is wanted, and there are few days when one cannot enjoy the outdoors and the sunshine.

Society there is none. The Romans are not a hospitable people, but one does not come to be with them. They are much divided into cliques and classes, and the great families content themselves in general with one great ball each year; very exclusive, and, if I may judge by hearsay of the foreigners who now and then attend, very dull. With two or three exceptions, the high nobility of Rome are as much of the Middle Ages as the old churches, and to the spiritual Roman they are mere shadows; we walk through and past them, and know not they are there. As a general thing, foreign society is organised apart. The old Roman aristocracy is divided into Blacks and Whites, Pope or King, and the two sections never mingle; the embassies from the same government to the Vatican and the Quirinal have no relations with each other, and the Blacks are not in the books of the embassies to the King, or the Whites invited to the receptions of those to the Pope. If the new-comer will see the world and can, he must choose under which colour he will take it, but in any case he will not find what in western lands is known as hospitality.

One of the most prominent English statesmen said to me one day, in Rome, that the life of public men was getting to be so laborious in the new political conditions in England that it would soon be a necessity to take refuge abroad from the constant demands of one's constituents, and that Italy, as the only available place of rest and refuge, would be more and more resorted to by them. Switzerland was useful only for a portion of the year; France was not far enough or restful enough; and so it must happen that Italy would become, to an increasing extent, the refuge of overworked statesmen. And of Italian cities, there is no question of the greater availability of Rome over all others. Florence is more interesting in the art of the Middle Ages; Venice holds the palm for its picturesqueness in the spring and early summer, but its winters are bleak and cheerless; Naples draws more from its surroundings, Sorrento and Capri, than it offers in itself; but Rome contains all that is most interesting in Italy. The superstition as to its sanitary condition is the bugbear which most militates against it. This runs back into the dark ages, but is unjustified by any statistics to which I can get access. In a residence of nearly a dozen years in the aggregate, and extending over a period of nearly thirty, I have never had in my family a single serious illness or a case of typhoid or malaria, and in my personal acquaintance I have never known half-a-dozen cases of intermittent or malarial fever, and not one of any gravity; while in a residence of five years in Florence we had eight cases of typhoid amongst seven persons. I have repeatedly stayed in Rome through the entire summer without any discomfort or inconvenience, and the late English ambassador, Lord Saville, was accustomed to spend his summers at the Embassy, saying that he found no place so comfortable all the year round as Rome. I have never met with a case of the so-called "pernicious" fever, and the physicians whom I know, and who attend foreigners mostly, bear a like testimony. Dr Drummond, who has practised here for years, says that he never saw a case. The instances of malarial fever I have known were similar to the intermittents of our own country—annoying, but not dangerous. The statistics of the Italian sanitary department are drawn up with the greatest care and exactitude, and for the purpose of improving the sanitary condition of the country, therefore with no reference to publication or to foreign opinion; and I have before me those of the deaths by malarial fevers for the commune of Rome, including the Campagna and the outlying towns and villages, Ostia and its marshes, to the sea, with all the malarial districts in the Ager Romanus; the division of the city from these being impracticable, as the peasants all come to the Roman hospitals for treatment. In these returns, out of a population of over 500,000, the total of deaths by malarial fevers was, in 1890, 308. The amelioration of the condition of public health under the government of Crispi can be judged from the diminution in the deaths, which has been from 600 in 1887, gradually and regularly, to 300 in the past year. With a system of thermal establishments such as the ancient Romans had, the deaths by malarial fevers would be still less; for there is no agency more effective in extirpating malaria than the vapour bath, yet there is not a tolerable Roman bath in Rome.

I am in continual receipt of letters asking if it is safe to come to Rome as early as October, or if it is safe to stay as late as May; and not unfrequently I meet people who think that the visit at any season is dangerous to life! Nothing is so invincible as superstition. If we leave Rome at all for the summer, it is only about the first of August, and we return by the end of September; not one-tenth of the population leaves, and the death-rate is lower in summer than in winter. From the first of November till the August rains begin to fall, the worst parts of the Campagna may safely be visited, if the sunset hours are avoided, and even in the intervening months the midday is free from danger; but from the first rains of August to the time of the setting in of frost, it is not wise to be in most parts of the Campagna towards sunset, though there are sections in which it is not safe to go to sleep at night in any season. The whole question of malaria in Italy is one of exaggerated importance. I have travelled in the worst parts of the Maremme, which are regarded as the most deadly and malarial of Italy, as late as the latter half of June, and have found the harvesters at work in gangs, and very few cases of fever anywhere; while at Grosseto, the capital of the Maremme, which the guide-books tell us is abandoned by the inhabitants on the first of May, I found the entire population on the ramparts listening to the band till late into the evening, and none had as yet gone to the hills, which they do only to a limited extent the first of July. I had an introduction to one family, the mother of which, whose life had always been passed in Grosseto, had never known, at the age of sixty, what intermittent fever was. I know of no district of Italy in which it is not practicable to travel ten months out of the twelve, if one takes the precautions not to sleep in a malarial locality, or drink water that is not known to be pure.

Typhoids are common in all great cities, but in Rome less so than in most cities of its size; and the returns to the sanitary authorities are a proof that their frequency is diminishing in proportion as the rigorous regulations are effective and evasion is prevented. The water supply of Rome is probably the best as to purity and the most abundant in quantity of any furnished to great cities. Typhoid very rarely occurs among the inhabitants of the better class except from drinking water at some wayside, or temporarily infected, spring. The main supply, that by the Acqua Marcia, is secure against pollution, and is everywhere accessible, so that no house need be without it. The sanitary laws are inflexible, and the tenant of a neglected house has always the remedy in his own hands. I have no hesitation in saying that a person in moderate circumstances, able to choose his quarters, can pass the months between September and July in Rome under as favourable conditions of health and comfort as in any city in Europe; and, with less precautions against the heat than in New York one must take against the cold, he may pass the entire year.

In summer, too, we have excellent seaside resorts—Anzio and Palo, and our hill country at Albano, Aricia, Nemi, Frascati, and the other *castelli*; and if there were a little enterprise in Italy, we should have summer resorts in the Abruzzi delightful in their sanitary and picturesque features, but this remains for future generations. Now a civilised man can hardly pass a day in any of the mountain villages or towns; filthy they are, beyond exaggeration. It is enough to insist on the advantages of Rome as a winter station, and as the fittest city of winter refuge for the exhausted and disabled, *hors de combat* in the battle of life, to whom political affinities are immaterial; for the refugees from the nervous pressure of America, the social, political, and business burdens of England; from the immitigable boredom of German life, as well as the glittering superficiality of Parisian: all such may meet here on the neutral ground of traditions, memories, and associations that antedate all our national divisions, and even all existing nationalities. *Quod est in votis.*

MARATHON AND ITS BRIGANDS

THE trip from Athens to Marathon is no joke, especially in summer, and when brigands are known to be sauntering unmolested along Mount Parnes, a night's walk away. Yet, when Messrs Goodenough and Cookson, American and English consular officials, escaped from Constantinople for a holiday, and stirred me out of my hot quarters at Athens to show them the lions, etc., of course it became necessary to put this excursion in the programme. It was in August of 1869, and we knew that there were brigands at Phylæ, and did not know that they were not nearer. In fact, the people of Athens were so panic-stricken that they would not go into the outskirts of the town in the evening; it was clear to the popular apprehension that we were besieged, and that the *roi des brigands*, whoever he might be for the time, was ruler of all the country round.

So, as our trip was to be in the nature of an invasion of an enemy's country, I decided to make it a surprise, and with strict injunctions of secrecy on all around, went, at nightfall of the day before we were to make the excursion, to the *Commandant de place* and asked an escort —"not that there was any use in it, but the strangers were anxious," etc. The Commandant stroked his moustache, expressed his sense of the high honour of having been permitted to make my acquaintance, offered me a cigarette, and we talked European politics, the Cretan insurrection, etc., and he assured me, as I rose to take my leave, that an escort of cavalry should be waiting at my door at 5 A.M. the next day. I went at 10 P.M. to the owner of horses and carriages and ordered a carriage for the early hour, and a relay of horses to be sent forward at once to the half-way station. I knew that if, even then, one of the friends of the brigands in town (by force of circumstances I should have said the carriage-owner, if I had been pressed to select one) should send word to his colleagues that four distinguished foreigners, of whom two certainly were ambassadors, were to start for Marathon on the morrow, they would not get the news before morning, and would not dare cross the plain by day, so that we could reach Athens again before they could get upon our road.

I awoke with the grey dawn and heard the hoofs of the troopers' horses clattering on the pavement in front of the house, and, running over to the hotel, found my friends wasting the precious coolness in deliberate breakfast. I inspected the horses, bullied the driver for having brought us the shabbiest carriage in Athens (by way of cutting down in advance his claim for backsheesh, or extra pay on any score), interjected a little Western celerity into the Eastern combination, and we started, picking up the escort *en route*. The road (that which conducts to Chalcis) is very good for a few miles, and we rattled along until we had passed Hymettus and emerged on the plains which slope towards Eubœa, when we turned sharp off by a bad waggon-track, rather than carriage-road, through the olive-orchards, and then through a pine-forest as solitary as the backwoods of America. No habitation, man, or grazing beast even, was to be seen; no tinkle of goat-bells to be heard. In the midst of this forest, by the side of a brook, seeming at first sight a succession of stagnant pools, bordered by a luxuriant growth of blackberries, oleanders, and rich grass, we found our relay waiting. There was no delay in changing, and about 10 A.M. we emerged from the wood on the marsh-bordered plain of Marathon.

The blue sea now breaks farther out than when the Persian keels fretted it and marked the sand that now lies hundreds of feet inland; and many acres of the marsh, where, doubtless, Persian bones and Persian trophies are bedded to this day, are now solid earth. We drove up to the mound through the maize-fields, and between the strips of vineyard, where the villagers of New Marathon were watching the early grapes; and having climbed the mound, made its circuit, and hunted for fragments of flint instruments, which form one of the items of interest at Marathon, we bought of the patriarch of the adjoining fields—who sat under a shelter of reeds guarding his riches, lest they took to themselves wings—a supply of water-melons, scarcely ripe grapes, and cantaloupes; each trooper confiscating one of the former, and quenching his thirst in the saddle. Then, having listened to the guide's tale of the battle, oft told, and ever growing in wondrous inequalities of heroism and butchery: and looked where he told us (and Murray, ever-to-be-consulted, confirmed,) that the Greeks held their position and the Persians landed: having, in short, "done" the place after the manner of the guide-book-led tourist, we drove back to the edge of the forest for shelter from the intense sun while we lunched.

I think that *timete Danaos* must be one of the things birched into us at school, for, with an immense liking for the race, I have an instinctive distrust of the preternatural shrewdness of the true Achaian, and our driver was of the genuine type, and had an uncanny way of looking across the bridge of his nose towards the mountains, which made me uneasy.

However, we lunched, drank copiously of good wine of Phalerum, while the driver pottered about his carriage and horses, to such good purpose that, when finally we started on the home road, we had not gone half-a-mile before the carriage came to a standstill, out of order. One of the wheels refused to revolve. Nothing was broken, so far as could be seen; but no efforts of all the persons concerned could make the wheel turn, or get it off its axle. The ever-to-be-suspected citizen of Athens begged us, with much serenity, to compose and assure ourselves, and be comfortable while he sent to Athens for another carriage. My misgivings coming to a head very rapidly, I asked him when the carriage would arrive; and he replied, in the happiest and most confident tone, that he *hoped* that it would get there by nightfall. "Very well," said I, "we will go and send it and you will stay and watch this carriage." The look of blank amazement and despair which came on his face as I pronounced this decision, as unappealable as a sentence of Minos, as he saw in my face and in the air of the commander of my squad when I pronounced it, was a revelation. Unhitching the horses, and dismounting two of the troopers, we rode back to the relay post at the little bridge, where the party of Lord Muncaster was captured not many months later, and there halted to wait for one of the dismounted men, who had been charged with a photographic camera, and had not kept up with us. Meanwhile, one of the troopers rode on to the next hamlet to see if some kind of trap could not be obtained; for, between foot-weariness and saddle-soreness, we were all desirous to change our method of locomotion. Our escort was thus diminished to two—the corporal and one private. The place was a capital one for an ambush, as the capturers of Lord Muncaster's party found it, and I looked into the thick trees growing each side of the brook on the bank overlooking it, and in the bed of it above us, with a certain nervousness, which increased when, after half-an-hour's waiting, the remaining trooper was sent back to look for the missing camera and its bearer.

There was nothing for it, however, but to wait till the escort reassembled; and we lit our cigarettes and lay down under the pine-trees. A circumstance that assured me somewhat was, that I found the troopers' carbines all unloaded (they were old-fashioned flint-lock smooth-bores) and that there was not a single cartridge in the company, from which I saw that they at least anticipated no danger. The corporal was a jolly, good-humoured veteran, whose air was that of a man ready for any emergency or danger. I asked him if he thought there was any ground for fear that, if we were obliged to wait long there, we might be carried off by some of the country-people, brigands *pro tempore*? He replied with the significant Greek negative, a silent pointing upward of the nose, accompanied by a slight arching of the brows, and, after another puff or two of his cigarette, said: "No; we know all the brigands, and generally know where they are. They could not stay here twenty-four hours without our knowing it, and we know that there have been none on this side of Pentelicus for several days. The common people here," he added, "are very honest and quiet, but very poor."

"Perhaps," ejaculated Cookson, "the one because

the other—put whichever you please as cause or effect in this country."

"I was a brigand myself once," said the corporal, after the pause in the conversation had lasted a few minutes; whereupon we all looked at him anew, and with a little more animation; and he added, as if in partial disclaimer, "but it was only for a few months."

"But how did it happen?" I asked; for though I knew that there had been brigands in the Cabinet in Greece, I did not suppose that the post of corporal in the mounted gendarmerie was a temptation to a gay rover who had felt the delight of outlawry.

"It was in this way," replied he. "I used to live in Acarnania, and, in one of the elections, there was a gentleman who had great influence in two or three of the villages, and who came from Athens to help the other side; and, as we knew that if these villages went against us we should lose the election, it was necessary to get rid of him. The chiefs of our party tried to draw him over to us; but, as he would not come, we had to get up a quarrel in the street, and he was killed. I was one of those who made the fight. I did not strike a blow, but I ran with the others to the mountains to wait till it all could be made right again. But, in spite of everything, the other side got the election and so we could not go back. If our men had been elected we should have been pardoned. So we went up to the Phthiotide and joined a band there, three of us; I stayed two years before I had a chance of getting back, and that came in the beginning of the Cretan insurrection, when many of the bands went over to fight with the Turks. When I did get back they made me corporal, as you see me; and, when there is any necessity to hunt the brigands, I generally go with the expedition, for I know all the roads. But this Government don't trouble them much. You see, General Soutzo, the Minister of War, has got an estate up in the brigands' country, and he knows very well that if he troubles them too much it will be plundered; and then it's no use running after them, for the moment an expedition starts they all go to the frontier, and are ready to cross over and get Turkish protection; and there are always some Turkish subjects in the bands, who make it all right with the guards."

"Did you ever make any prizes while you were in the band?" I asked.

"No great gentlemen; only a few Wallachian and Bulgarian merchants. The bands don't like to trouble Franks, unless it is a lord or some very rich man who can pay a big ransom, for the affair makes so much more trouble when it is a Frank, and they get pursued and have to leave their families for a long time: and it don't do," he ejaculated, with a shrug.

"But have they families with them?" I asked.

"Perhaps," suggested Cookson, "they have as many as they have hiding-places."

The corporal's nose went up in the air with a

quiet expression of his evident feeling that we did not in the least understand the respectability of the kleptic calling, as he replied, "No; they always stay near their families, except when the expeditions are out, and get their supplies from their relations. You must know that when Comoundouros was First Minister, there were some bands in the Morea, and the nomarch of Argos, the same who caught Kitzos, sent all the families of the brigands over to the islands, and they had to come in and surrender in a few weeks; all but one band near Patras, and they would have come too, if Bulgaris had not come in First Minister, and sent the nomarch away, because they said he violated the Constitution. That is what makes the country so poor, this changing the Ministers all the time; and the King, he's of no use, only costs thirty million drachmas a year"; and the politician born shrugged his shoulders with an expression of contempt for such a state of things. He proceeded, however, after a moment :—" The chiefs never allow the members of their bands to marry or steal women if they are already married, because it always makes trouble, and the women betray the bands to punish them. One of our band one day stole a very pretty girl from a village near Lamia; and when the chief ordered him to take her back, and he refused and threatened to leave the band, the chief shot him dead, and sent the girl home. Her father paid us well by giving information of a rich Bulgarian wool-merchant, who was buying wool in the mountains near Lamia, and we carried him off, and got twenty thousand drachmas ransom. That was the best capture we made while I was in the band. We tried to catch an English lord once who was going over to the Eubœa; but some of the people told Mr. Noel, an English gentleman who lives at Achmet Aga, and he sent the lord warning."

"How did you know he was a lord?" I asked.

"Oh, one of the band had a cousin who was a waiter in the hotel where the lord lived, and he sent us word that he was coming, and that he had so much money that he did not know how to spend it; for he bought all kinds of antiquities for whatever price people asked him, and gave backsheesh like a fool. If we had caught him we should have made him pay ten thousand pounds ransom, and then we should have gone over the frontier and bought property in Epirus, and become Turkish subjects. Ten thousand pounds is a good deal of money," he appended, by way of reflection.

Here he got up and walked across the bridge to the brink of the opposite bank, and listened if he could catch any sound of the horse of the trooper sent after the missing footman. Nothing. What could the matter be? Had they both been gobbled up by the brigands? Their firearms, I knew, were not loaded, and they could not even fire a shot of warning for us. There was, however, nothing to do but wait; and wait we did. The troopers' saddles were very bad; one of the party was no horseman, and was already both footsore and saddle-sore, for we had come twelve miles since the break-down; another was a cripple—and to get back to Athens afoot was, therefore, to two of us impossible. Then we had only three available horses: the corporal being too portly and equestrian to get home afoot, two of the gendarmes being away with their horses, and the man who had brought the relay horses having started for Athens on one of his spare beasts to hurry up the other carriage. Of the remaining three, none had saddles; and the two which had brought us from Marathon were thoroughly jaded. We had ten or twelve miles still to go, and the prospect was not a pleasant one.

Presently the trooper who had been sent back came clattering along with the news that the missing comrade was not to be found. He had ridden back to the carriage, and found no trace of him on the road. The other, sent after a vehicle, had not returned, and it was now nearly mid-afternoon. We all grew nervous and irritable, and I confidently expected to see the dirty fustanella appear in the bushes around. Cookson began, in Stamboul Greek, with strong English accent, to abuse the Government and Greece in general, to which the corporal replied imperturbably, for the Greeks are too much in the habit of hearing their State berated to think much about it; and it sometimes occurs to me that, as they do really, in general, receive more abuse than they deserve, it may have had the effect of diminishing the self-respect which man or nation must possess, to win the respect of others. So the corporal re-echoed the epithets levelled at the Ministers, and abused the King, who, he said, might better matters if he were not so given up to his favourites. It is hard quarrelling with a man who takes your side in the quarrel, and we had to stop berating the Government, as the corporal beat us out and out in virulence.

"But tell me, Stavros," said I, at length, "what would you do if you were Minister of War to put down brigandage?"

"Do!" replied he, the feather of imagination tickling his importance so that he became really ministerial in dignity. "I would very soon stop it. I would make the villages pay all the ransoms which were taken in their territory. I would do as the nomarch of Argos did, and send the families of all the brigands out to live in the islands, and I would have all brigands shot as soon as taken, instead of being sent as they are now, to the Palamidi, to wait for a new election, and then be pardoned to go into the provinces to make influence. But the Turkish Government must work with ours, or there cannot be an end to it. Why, not a year ago, when we were going to fight the Turks about the *Ennosis*, and Hobart Pacha went to Syra to take her, I was with an expedition to look at the boundary near Arta, and the brigands took two of our officers who slept in a village without sentinels, and carried them over the frontiers, and kept them in the Turkish guardhouse for ransom, and the Turkish captain had part of the ransom. You might as well attempt to shut all the fish into Piræus harbour as to try to shut the brigands off from the boundary. If all the lazy regulars who live in the barracks of Athens, and do nothing but set guard at the palace and march about town, were put on the boundary, they wouldn't keep a man from passing when he liked. But they might watch the villagers, to keep the brigands from coming down to get bread or powder, or from capturing any one, and in time they would be starved out. But they must send the families away — that will stop them quicker than anything else."

"But," I said, "that is illegal—it's against the Constitution."

"Bah!" said the indignant soldier, "we hear of the Constitution when it serves the Ministers —never when it protects the people. The Constitution is like the middle of a fast*—you may do what you like with it. There are sixty brigands in chains now in the Palamidi, and I'll lay a wager that forty will be pardoned in a year, and yet the Constitution does not permit the pardoning of a brigand without the Chambers. I know fellows who have been released two or three times. It is all very well to talk of constitutions and laws; but I think that Ministers

* The practice of many in Greece is to keep only the first and last weeks of the long fasts. Strict devotees keep the whole, 146 days of each year.

make them for their own good, and keep them when they like. In my opinion, the law that does the work is the law we want, and if I was Minister I would make law enough to do what I wanted. I know a butcher in Athens who has a brother a brigand in a band near Galaxidi, and he keeps the band informed of all people going there; and I suppose if we put him in prison, as he deserves, there would be a great talk about the Constitution; but, if I had my way, I would lock him up in the Palamidi, and his lawyers with him. Your Constitutions may be all very well in other countries, but——" and he finished by a thumb over his shoulder. "Constitution!" he ejaculated again, after a little, with a contemptuous shrug, as though his ideas had been rumbling away in some inner cavern, and had come out in an echo.

It grew late when the man sent in search of a vehicle returned, saying that nothing was to be found. The missing man must be abandoned, and we must push on as we could, hoping, on the high road, to fall in with some means of transport. The two troopers gave up their horses cheerfully in view of backsheesh, the two best of the carriage-horses bore the other two of us, and without other mishaps we journeyed along as far as the road, when at a half-fortified metochi, we found a butcher's cart, which, filled with straw and packed densely with the four of us, in addition to the guide and driver, served to bring us with much pain to Athens, where we arrived about 10 P.M. The missing trooper was waiting at the metochi.

The next day, about sunset, I happened to meet the carriage returning, and had the curiosity to ask our driver what was the matter.

"Only a nail which had got between the axle and wheel and would not let it turn."

"Ah!" I said, "how did the nail get there?"

The driver shrugged his shoulders with a bland smile, which might be understood to mean anything you pleased. *I* took it to mean that he knew when and why the nail got in; and, had I been Stavros' model Minister, I should certainly have sent him to the Palamidi forthwith.

MY EXPERIENCE IN A GREEK QUARANTINE

HAVING occasion during the summer of 1865 to go from Crete to European terra-firma, I was obliged to go to Syra, the entrepôt of the Levant, to take passage in the Austrian Lloyd's steamer; but as the cholera panic and the restrictions laid on the steamers from all Turkish ports had virtually stopped regular communication with Greek ports, I took a passage in an English "Brixham schooner" which had come out with a cargo of soda, etc. Our island had had no case of cholera, and indeed has never been visited by it; its general healthfulness was all that could be desired by the most exacting Board of Health, and as, moreover, we were fortified with English, Turkish, and Greek bills of health, I anticipated at the worst a detention of four or five days previous to being permitted to land.

We had a charming run of thirty odd hours, with just wind enough to make a landsman love the sea, and sighting Syra in the morning, stood directly in for the port. Half-a-mile off the mole-head we met a man-of-war's boat, the Greek blue and white stripes flying out from the stern, and received a most peremptory warning to go no nearer, fearfully shouted from a safe distance; and on learning that we were from a Turkish port, the officer ordered us off to Delos for eleven days' quarantine, not daring even to look at our bill of health or hear any protest or explanations.

Those who have been at Syra may remember to the west of that port, and about ten miles away, a low, bare, and rocky island, which few people ever visit, and on which only two or three herdsmen live. On closer inspection one finds that what seemed to be one is really two islands, the larger called sometimes Rhenée, and sometimes the greater Delos, the smaller the true Delos, site of the famous temple of Apollo. In a bay on the south-eastern side of the former, the schooner cast anchor, and the so-called lazaretto being only an insignificant collection of huts, built of rough boards, I elected to perform quarantine on board. In fact, the bare, dry, even burnt look of the island, without a shrub, a spring, or a living thing on it except a few *guardiani* and some luckless passengers of an English steamer which had preceded us by a few days, gave small hope of being able to pass eleven days of idleness endurably, in the heat of midsummer, where the sun is as fervent as it is on the south side of a Greek island. The steamer was from Alexandria, with over two hundred passengers on board, mostly Syriotes and other Greeks flying from the cholera, then in the beginning of its fury at that city; therefore they were most naturally put into quarantine. Their term was fourteen days, I believe, of which nearly a week had passed without any symptoms of sickness of any kind. We were near enough to hail across to her on still days and hear the complaints of the captain roared at sympathetic ears in good broad English, and witness by eye and ear the facts I am about to narrate, which I challenge the most patriotic and mendacious inhabitant of Syra to contradict.

The captain of the steamer having, like myself, only calculated on a few days' observation, had provided himself with sufficient stores for the time for his few cabin passengers, the great bulk of those on board being deck passengers, who provide themselves with food for the voyage. These had been exhausted soon after their arrival at quarantine; and the captain, praying in vain for supplies from the authorities of Syra, began to give out his ship's supplies; for it was impossible, as he said, to see the poor people starve. But these supplies, abundant for his proper ends, would go but a little way in feeding that hungry multitude, and were threatened with exhaustion before the townspeople should awaken their Christianity from its sleep of, I imagine, about seventeen centuries. The captain appealed in vain to them to save their countrymen from starvation. They were not bound, they said, to provide food for people because they found them in quarantine. So the captain gave out all his stores, little by little, and shouted across to us to know if we had any to spare. The *Sylph* carried a crew of five men, and we naturally had two or three barrels of hard bread and salt beef stowed away for emergencies; and though what we could give them, with proper regard to our own needs, could be little more than a few hours' respite from starvation, it was impossible to withhold it.

The captain was an incarnate protest, a deck-walking imprecation on the miserly authorities of Syra. The people in his ship were not his own countrymen, but Greeks; he was under no obligation to provide a mouthful for one of them; they had no money to buy, and he had no authority to buy for them except from his own funds—to have done which he must have been a Roman prince or an English banker. So he wrote, and begged, and protested. He wrote to the English consul, Mr. Lloyd, and Mr. Lloyd stormed at the nomarch and demarch by turns in vain. The Syriotes would not send, and the consul could not, save a little for the captain and crew; and provisions were not only not supplied by the Board of Health, but permission to carry them off to the steamer was denied those who would have taken them, so great was the panic at the idea of communication with the ship. Mr. Lloyd succeeded now and then in sending a small supply by the *guarda-costa*, and they bought now and then a kid of the herdsmen on the "clean" part of the island, at exorbitant rates. But they, too, finally refused to communicate; and then the captain wrote to the consul—I saw the letter afterwards—"For three days my men have had no bread, and two of them have gone raving mad." Amongst the cabin passengers was a Frenchwoman, pregnant and near her confinement; for her the captain begged for a doctor or nurse in vain—none would venture; and when the time was come the poor mother had only the kindly care of the captain and her fellow-passengers, among whom was no woman or person competent to care for her. Fortunately, she passed through her trial safely.

In the meanwhile, Mr. Lloyd kept up his protests and remonstrances to people and Government—protested against the inhumanity and the illegality of the whole thing—begged for relief to deaf ears: "Better," they said, "that a few should suffer than that forty thousand should incur the peril of cholera. To allow people to carry provisions to the island was to run danger of communication with contagion." The only reply of any significance that Mr. Lloyd got was a threat of burning his house over his head if he persisted in attempting to bring cholera into Syra.

We, faintly realising the nature of this little turmoil, lay quietly under the intense sun waiting the lapse of time. The Greeks on the steamer might starve, but we were perhaps thankful that they were only Greeks; *we* should wear through well enough, and then be free. Mr. Lloyd finally wrote to Athens; the Government at Athens ordered an examination; and then the demos,

EXPERIENCE IN A GREEK QUARANTINE

under compulsion, voted meagre supplies to their famished countrymen.

But our fates were merciless. A few days, very few, before the steamer's time had expired, a ship arrived from Alexandria which actually had the cholera on board! Twenty or more had died and were thrown overboard on the voyage, as we afterwards learned, and several more were sick. As she came into the quarantine anchoring-ground and cast anchor, she dragged some distance, and seemed in a fair way to drift against the armed cutter which was doing duty as *guarda-costa* and *capo-guardiano*. The brave captain—(I hope he wasn't a sailor)—ran out his guns and prepared to sink the ship and all on board, lest she should come into contact with him. That scene is one I shall never forget and hardly ever forgive: the huddled passengers driven on deck by the pestilence and heat, and, doubtless, already in a frenzy of fear from the perils within, found themselves met on the threshold of deliverance from their awful fellow-voyager by the open mouths of Greek carronades. Women shrieked and men howled with fright; all prayed, supplicating the gods and the captain. The *guarda-costa* people were in a worse panic, if possible — shouted orders and counter-orders, ran out a gun and ran it in again, threatened, prayed and cursed, as though doom was on them. This horror of the cholera seemed to have become a madness in the Greek mind. Our sailors gave the wretches the benefit of much good and strong English, which I fear was sadly wasted, and would have been equally so had it been equally good Greek; but I noticed that our *guardiano* was stricken with fear at the bare idea of the vicinity of the infected ship. What the extent of the contagion was we knew not, of course; but the hurrying and trepidation of the people on board, and in the boat which came alongside, made it evident that something unusual was going on. The boat lay far off, and the officers shouted very loudly; and we heard afterwards from the quarantine-boat that there were four or five dead of cholera on board, whom they wanted to send on shore to be buried, but this was refused as dangerous! then to be permitted to sink them in the sea—this was still less to be allowed. They begged for a doctor—no one would go: *guardiani* even would not go on board for any compensation, and they rowed away, leaving her to her fate. We shortly after received an intimation that by reason of this new arrival all ships in quarantine at that time must stay fourteen days more!

My own wrath at Greek inhumanity had been already so largely excited that I could get no angrier at this new tyranny—in fact, I thought more of the steamer and its already half-starved, and even, in some cases, dying people, than of myself; and if I had had the pestilence in the hollow of my hand, I should, I fear, have visited Syra as Egypt never was visited. But the most appalling thought was of that luckless ship with Death holding revel on her, and the living bound to the dead.

EXPERIENCE IN A GREEK QUARANTINE 47

Here was the ship of the ancient mariner, in sooth—anchored only, but with anchors almost useless on that tranquil sea, the fiery sun above, and the glassy water below, and nothing to break that awful monotony but the merciless quarantine-boat coming to ask and refuse. We could see the people on the ship gather on the forecastle and in the rigging, looking out to the land, which, brown and dry as it was, was to them a refuge. The second and the third day came, and the dead multiplied, until ten or a dozen corpses were on board. Still no physician, no landing, no burial even; and the plague-stricken ship and its dying cargo lay still under the August sun. The third day the crew received permission to put the bodies overboard, tied with ropes, that they might not drift away and carry to some accursed Greek community the plague it merited. I may be unjust, but those days have made me detest and abhor the very name of Syra and its people. We saw the dead lowered overboard, one by one, and with glasses could see them floating alongside, horrible to sight and fancy.

I am only dealing with facts—facts which will be confirmed by the testimony of many who passed those broiling August days in that quarantine. No physician could be found in Syra who had humanity enough to hear the cry of that suffering company, or venture on the plague-stricken ship. They latterly got permission to bury the dead, all but one mother and child, who drifted loose, and were cast on some unknown shore, or fed the fishes; subsequently a Danish physician came, a volunteer from — I regret to say I know not where, nor even do I know his name. I did not think then to enable myself to render him the honour he deserves; and finally the sick were landed. There had been a hundred and forty passengers on board when the ship left Alexandria, and there were over a hundred when she came to quarantine — the untouched remaining on board until they were attacked in their turn, and were carried ashore to die. Their provisions, too, were failing, and at last starvation came to help the pestilence.

I sought distraction and pastime amongst the sailors, of whom two had attracted my attention during the run over. One of them I judged to be an American at first sight, the incarnation of "go-a-head" and nervous energy. I had seen him at the wheel the first day out, as I sat aft taking my fruit after dinner, and tempted him to affability by a huge slice of melon, which he ate without ever taking his eye for more than an instant from the course of the schooner. The next day they were apples that broke the silence; when, abruptly turning round to me, he asked if I was a freemason. He was, and evidently did not understand how one could treat a sailor with courtesy or kindness without some such motive as that mystic brotherhood is supposed to furnish. He wore a black wide-awake crowded close down to his eyes, which looked sharp out from under black, clear-drawn eyebrows. His nose was prominent, pointed,

EXPERIENCE IN A GREEK QUARANTINE 49

and straight, and his mouth full of decision; lips close-pressed, and chin small and slightly retreating. He carried his head habitually a little forward, as if on the look-out, and reminded me in his *ensemble* more of a clipper than anything I ever saw in flesh. He was taciturn, however, and absolutely refused to talk of himself. The other, who responded to the name of Bill, was certainly one of the best examples of the English sailor I have ever met—robust, thick-set, with large brain and full beard, a frank blue eye, and an off-hand manner familiar to all who permitted it, but respectful to the highest degree, and speaking the English of a man who had had some education. In the first days of our imprisonment he had surprised me not a little by offering to lend me some old numbers of reviews and magazines, written on the margins of which I found some shrewd comments, and with some bits of drawing. I am not going to write his story, and shall not repeat what I learned of a life ruined by an uncontrollable spirit of adventure and unimproved opportunities; I have only to do with him now as he wove himself into the web of our quarantine life.

It was from Bill that I learned what I first knew of Aleck; that he was, as I supposed, an American, had been in the Confederate service, and had even served on the *Alabama*. After finding out so much, I tried hard to make him talk about himself, but in vain. He was respectful, but not communicative on any subject, and least so on himself. But the new excitement of the cholera-ship and its horrors made a certain difference. I certainly felt more like getting near my fellow-men, and they, and especially Aleck, were more oblivious of the difference between them and me. The immediate cause of the breaking of the ice was the sight of a poor woman standing on the poop of the cholera-ship as she swung towards us from her anchorage, before a slight easterly air, that brought the woman's voice down to us in supplications which we could from time to time partially distinguish, and which were for bread, bread, bread! We could see others on board climbing on the bulwarks, standing on the poop or forecastle, according to the end of the ship which drifted nearest us; but we could hear no other voice, though we doubted not that many were joined with hers. Beside her we saw, later, another female figure, whom, by the aid of the glass, I believed I could make out to be her daughter. The latter made no sound that we could hear, but sat mutely or stood with her arm around the other, while ever and anon we heard that heartrending cry, "*Psomí! psomí!*" (bread! bread!). At sunset that day we were all together on the forecastle, better friends through our common pity. We proposed to our taciturn *guardiano* to send some bread on board the ship, but he absolutely refused to lend himself to any such risk of contagion, and forbade any attempt to communicate either with the ship or the shore where the sick were; and, to tell the

EXPERIENCE IN A GREEK QUARANTINE 51

truth, it was not pleasant to contemplate the chances of being put in quarantine for an additional indefinite term, for having, even in a kindly work, come in real or fancied contact with the disease. But as the authority of the *guardiano* was absolute, we could do nothing in the matter openly, though it was determined in council by us three to do something in some way, if relief was not brought soon.

From the forecastle next morning we saw in the early light the two hapless creatures in the same position. Bill, looking over into the water thoughtfully, asked if there were many sharks in those waters. I replied that I had never seen but one, inquiring why he asked. "Why," said he, "I think I could get some grub over to those women if you could manage the *guardiano*." "It isn't much of a swim," I replied, "but as to carrying the prog, you will find that more difficult." "Well," said he, "I have carried a pretty good load in the water before now, and can float enough to keep those women from starving. I lived in the Sandwich Islands once, and though I don't stand out of the water like a Kanaka, I have carried my clothes on my head many a mile without wetting them, and a few pounds of bread won't sink me." Here his eye twinkled as if he had a story to tell, and I waited for it. "I commanded a lorcha transport during the last war in China," he began, after a moment, "and one day, while we were in Canton, I was walking through one of the streets with my mate, an Englishman, and we stopped to look in a joss-house. There was a joss there of pure silver, about fourteen inches high, and I made up my mind to have him. We two were the only Europeans on board, and the first dark stormy night we took the boat and went ashore well armed. The joss-house had no guard but the priests, and the night was so bad that we broke the door down and got in without the outsiders knowing it, and carried the joss off easily enough; but the next day we had row enough to pay for it. Every vessel in the river was searched, and if I had had him on board he would have been found and we should have caught it, for the officers were in earnest about it, and the Chinese in a fury. I knew there would be the d——l to pay in the morning, so I put a cord around his neck, and went down and hung him to the lower pintle of the rudder, and left him there till the hue-and-cry was over, and then brought him up. He weighed forty-two pounds. I think I could do more in this case than then." "Do it then," said I; "I'll help you all I can: but we won't let the captain or any of the men know of it!" "Oh, I'll put that all right," said Aleck. "Jones has the first watch to-night, and I'll change with him; and as for the *guardiano*, he's a sleepy cuss, and I reckon won't give himself the trouble to look on deck after he turns in—he never has, any way; and if you'd like to keep watch with me, sir, I think we can manage it." "But, Bill," I added, "look out for the *guarda-costa*: if they see anything in the

EXPERIENCE IN A GREEK QUARANTINE 53

water moving between the vessels, they'll fire at it, certainly." "That won't trouble me," replied the imperturbable tar. "I have run the blockade in the American war thirteen times, and had bigger balls than that fellow can throw whizzing about my head, and fired by better gunners than they have got aboard there. Why, sir, we ran almost into one of their Monitors one night, and had eight 15-inch shot fired at us without being hit; and in all the thirteen trips in and out we never were hit but once, and then the ball only took off the head of the look-out forward."

And so we arranged it that Bill should swim off to the ship as soon as it was dark, and trusting to fortune to get the provisions aboard without discovery, we were to hang overboard a light for him to swim back to.

"That ship reminds me," said Bill, after a long pause, "of a trip I made once in an English ship to Senegal. We went up the river to load, and while we lay there waiting for cargo to come down, we had one of the worst yellow fevers break out on the ship I ever saw. The first man who was taken with it died in three hours, and that day two more were taken and died before dark, and in three days we lost all but seven of the crew, one after the other—not one was sick more than six hours—and then the mate was taken sick. The first thing I knew of it was that he said to me, 'Bill, give me a good glass of grog, and fill my pipe; I want one good smoke and a drink before I die.' 'Oh, nonsense,' says I, 'you are no more likely to die than I am.' 'I know very well I have got it,' said he; 'and when I am dead bury me deep enough so that the land crabs can't dig me up.' Sure enough he died that afternoon, and we took him ashore before night and buried him in a good deep grave. In two days more there were only the captain and I alive on the ship. And there we lay ten days till we heard that an English man-of-war was off the mouth of the river, and the captain sent a native boat down to ask him to send up men to work the ship out of the river. The man-of-war sent word that they wouldn't send men up the river, but if we could work her down with natives, they would give us men to get the ship home to England, and so we got out, but a deuce of a time we had of it getting down. I suppose they feel on that ship pretty much as I did those ten days."

All day long we heard at intervals that pitiful cry, "Bread! bread!" faintly coming over the water. It was more tolerable than the day before, because we knew that relief would go with nightfall. And so, as the dark came, we made up a packet of hard bread with a little cold meat and a bottle of wine, and binding it securely between Bill's shoulders, and with a pointed stick on top of it, in case, as he said, "a shark should want to take the prog from him," he slipped down into the water, stripped to his drawers, and struck out for the cholera-ship so quietly that you might have thought it a little school of guard-fish.

We sat on the forecastle watching and waiting. I said nothing, and where two are together and one will not talk, the other sometimes will. Aleck finally broke silence with—"Women are mighty curious things. I'll bet that old one don't touch a mouthful till t'other has eaten, and I don't believe she would have made half the fuss she did if she had been alone. In the beginning of the American war I belonged to a regiment of mounted riflemen, and we were sent into Eastern Tennessee, where there was a good deal of bushwhacking about that time. We were picketed one day in a line about two miles long across country, and I was on the extreme left. I took my saddle off, holsters and all, and hung it on a branch of a peach-tree, and my carbine on another. We knew there were no Yankees near, and so I was kind o' off guard, eating peaches. By-and-by I saw a young woman coming down to where I was, on horseback. She wanted to know if there were many of the boys near, and if they would buy some milk of her if she took it down to them. I said I thought they would, and took about a quart myself; and as she hadn't much more, I emptied the water out of my canteen and took the rest. Says she, 'If you'll come up to the house yonder, I've got something better than that: you may have some good peach brandy —some of your fellows might like a little.' I said I'd go, and she says, 'You needn't take your saddle or carbine, it's just a step, and they are safe enough here—there's nobody about.' So I mounted bareback, and she led the way. When we passed the bars where she came in, she says, 'You ride on a step, and I'll get down and put up the bars.' I went on, and as she came up behind, she says pretty sharp, 'Ride a little faster, if you please.' I looked round, and she had a revolver pointed straight at my head, and I saw that she knew how to use it. I had left everything behind me like a fool, and had to give in and obey orders. 'That's the house, if you please,' she says, and showed me a house in the edge of the woods a quarter of a mile away. We got there, and she told me to get down and eat something, for she was going to give me a long ride—into the Yankee lines, about twenty miles away. Her father came out and abused me like a thief, and told me that he was going to have me sent into the Federal lines to be hung. It seems he had had a son hung the week before by some of the Confederates, and was going to have his revenge out of me. I ate pretty well, for I thought I might need it before I got any more, and then the old fellow began to curse me and abuse me like anything. He said he would shoot me on the spot if it wasn't that he'd rather have me hung; and instead of giving me my own horse, he took the worst one he had in his stables, and they put me on that with my feet tied together under his belly. Luckily they didn't tie my hands, for they thought I had no arms, and couldn't help myself; but I always carried a small revolver in my shirt bosom. The girl kept too sharp

EXPERIENCE IN A GREEK QUARANTINE 57

watch on me for me to use it. She never turned her revolver from me, and I knew that the first suspicious move I made I was a dead man. We went about ten miles in this way, when my old crow-bait gave out and wouldn't go any farther. She wouldn't trust me afoot, and so had to give up her own horse, but she kept the bridle in her own hands, and walked ahead with one eye turned back on me, and the revolver cocked with her finger on the trigger, so that I never had a chance to put my hand in my bosom. We finally came to a spring, and she asked me if I wanted to drink: I didn't feel much like drinking, but I said yes, and so she let me down. I put my head down to the water, and at the same time put my hand down where the revolver was, and pulled it forward where I could put my hand on it easily; but she was on the watch and I couldn't pull it out. I mounted again, and the first time she was off her guard a little I fired, and broke the arm she held the pistol in. 'Now,' says I, 'it's my turn: you'll please get on that horse and we'll go back.' She didn't flinch or say a word, but got on the horse, and I tied her legs as they had mine, and we went back to the house. The old man he heard us come up to the door and looked out of the window. He turned as pale as a sheet and ran for his rifle. I knew what he was after, and pushed the door in before he was loaded. Says I, 'You may put that shooting-iron down and come with me.' He wasn't as brave as the girl, but it was no use to resist, and he knew it; so he came along. About half-way back we met some of our fellows who had missed me, and come out to look me up. They took them both, and——" He paused a moment, and lowering his tone, added, "I don't know what they did with them, but I know d—— well what they would have done with me." I replied, after a pause, "I suppose they hanged them both?" Aleck nodded his head without looking up, and seemed anxious to drop the subject.

"But," said I, rather disposed to work the vein of communicativeness, but not anxious to hear any more *such* adventures, "I thought you had been in the Confederate navy?" "I was," said Aleck. "I was with Semmes everywhere he went; I was in the naval brigade and blockade-running, and on the *Alabama* all the while he commanded her." "But not when she sank, I suppose?" I rejoined. "*Well*, I was, and was picked up with him by the *Deerhound*." "It was a pretty sharp fight, wasn't it?" I suggestingly asked. "It was that," replied Aleck, but he didn't care about enlarging. "I suppose it was the eleven-inch shells that did her business?" "Oh, no," said he, coming to a kind of confessional, "we never had any chance; we had no gunners to compare with the *Kearsage's*. Our gunners fired by routine, and when they had the gun loaded, fired it off blind. They never changed the elevation of their guns all the fight, and the *Kearsage* was working up to us all the while, taking

EXPERIENCE IN A GREEK QUARANTINE 59

advantage of every time she was hid by smoke to work a little nearer, and then her gunners took aim for every shot." "Then it isn't true that the *Alabama* tried to board the *Kearsage*?" "No, *sir*; she did her best to get away from her from the time the fight commenced: we knew well that if we got in range of her Dahlgren howitzers she would sink us in ten minutes." "But," I asked, "don't you believe that Semmes supposed he would whip the *Kearsage* when he went out to fight her?" "No: he was bullied into it, and took good care to leave all his valuables on shore, and had a life-preserver on through the fight. I saw him put it on, and I thought if it was wise in him it wouldn't be foolish in me, and I put one on too. When Semmes saw that the ship was going down, he told us all to swim who could, and was one of the first to jump into the water, and we all made for the *Deerhound*. I was a long way ahead of Semmes, and when I came up to the *Deerhound's* boat they asked me if I was Semmes before they would take me in. I said I wasn't, and then they asked me what I was on the *Alabama*. Said I, 'No matter what I was on the *Alabama*, I shall be a dead man soon if you don't take me in.' They asked me again if I was an officer or a seaman, and wouldn't take me in until I told them that I was an officer." "But," said I, "did they actually refuse to pick up common seamen, and leave them to drown?" "They did that," replied he wrathfully, "and as soon as they had Semmes on board they made tracks as fast as they knew how, and left everybody else to drown or be picked up by the *Kearsage*."

"Time to show the light, I reckon," said Aleck, after his ebullition had subsided, and proceeded to put over the bows the light agreed on. Half-an-hour after Bill had started on his voyage we heard his whistle from below the forechains, and heaving him a line brought him in cautiously. He slipped down to change his clothing and add to it, and then came up to render an account of his doings. He had, as he anticipated, found more difficulty in getting on board the ship than in getting to it. He had found the poor women on the quarter-deck — all order and shipkeeping abandoned, and no look-out anywhere. The passengers were sleeping on deck or sitting around it, moaning and weeping. He dared not call to the women for fear of disturbing the *guardiani* and of attracting the attention of the other passengers, to whom his small supply would have been but a mouthful. He swam round and round looking for a loose rope's-end in vain, and finally did what we should have supposed certain to lead to his discovery — climbed up the cable and over the bows, throwing over his shoulders the first garment he found on the disorderly deck, and slowly walked the whole length of the ship: when, having deposited the provisions at the side of the unfortunate ones, signifying that they were to inform no one and keep them to them-

EXPERIENCE IN A GREEK QUARANTINE 61

selves, as well as his few words of Greek would let him, he dropped overboard by a line from the quarter, and leaving them in mute and motionless wonder, came back as quietly as he had gone. Bill couldn't resist the temptation next morning of waving a big white cloth at the ship, a signal which attracted the immediate attention and suspicion of our watchful *guardiano*, who, with an effervescence of useless Greek, delivered his mind on the subject of *contumacia* and communication, at which we all laughed: we felt merrier that morning than for many days past.

In fact, though we saw for several days more the boat going back and forwards from the ship to the shore, and knew that they went to bury the dead, could see them buried even with our glasses, we never felt so oppressed by the horror of it since Bill's chivalric swim. We finished without other incident our appointed two weeks, and had soon the satisfaction of knowing that public clamour had obliged Syra to recognise the claims of humanity, and send food to the starving.

We had to undergo a five days' "observation" behind the lighthouse island off the port, in company with the English steamer, which was, moreover, threatened with a third fortnight; which she escaped only by the energetic remonstrances of the British consul, backed up by the Legation at Athens, who persuaded the central government to send orders to Syra that the steamer should be admitted to pratique. A Greek man-of-war was accordingly sent from the Piræus to Syra with a commission to ascertain the truth of the complaints of Mr. Lloyd, and finding them well-founded, ordered the admittance of the steamer to pratique; but so great was the terror of the population and the timidity of the commission, that the latter ceded to the threats of a revolution, and compromised on admitting the passengers to the lazaretto of Syra and sending the ship away. If all these things are not recorded in the chronicles of that city, they are in the minds of many who were martyrs to the inhuman cowardice of Syra, and who will bear me testimony *that every occurrence of which public recognition could be taken in the above narrative is strictly true.* As for the yarns, I tell them, as nearly as I can remember, as they were told me, and—believe them.

AN AMERICAN'S REVERIE OVER LONDON

WHAT survives of the seven wonders of the world may mainly be seen in London, itself the eighth and greatest, not only for what of the Old World and older times it holds, but for the living, growing marvel that it is, the highest achievement of the agglomerating human spirit. With all the years I have known it, and the times I have been in and out of it, I find at every return that I scarcely know how great it is, or realise how wise and how wicked, how noble and how stolid. Mighty and wealthy beyond any dreams of Arabian Nights; wrapping in its tortuous folds all extremes of human existence; by turns, a city of palaces, and the nest of the highest and divinest human impulse, and the smoke-blackened, fog-wrapped, dingy, gloomy capital of Cimmeria; plague latent in its alleys, and utter destitution driving their people to death and all degradation in clouds like the flies that perish—it seems the very focus of life-and-death ferment, quickening and releasing at once what is divinest and most infernal in the human heart, and ripening both as no other city built by human hands has done.

Visit it for the first time from the south, if possible, in the autumn, and towards the close of day, when the grey incertitude lies on the mighty city. You will have come through the lovely country of Kent, Hampshire, and Surrey,—garden of England,—the little compact villages twinkling by the railway side, the ever-green fields chasing the parks, and the parks following the downs, in an unbroken succession of lovely landscapes; then the villages come closer together, and you see the houses begin to lose their pagan aspect and grow up storeys higher—villas—suburb houses, miles of suburbs with intervals yet to become city; and then you come on the outskirts of the world's metropolis, no longer suburbs pushing off for better air, but low, dingy haunts of labour and poverty, packed and involved in economic leaseholds on earth's surface—scarcely more than graveyard room. You look down into the streets—into the windows, down chimney-pots even; and the din of unnumbered streets, the smoke of myriad chimneys, and the twinkle of lamps as the very stars of heaven for their multitude, come up to you whirling along dizzily above it all. You hear the hum of the world below you, and, as far as the eye can catch the gleam of gas-light through the space around, there is an unbroken, endless wilderness of houses. Wider streets yawn and send up a sudden, stronger pulsation of sound, but no change beyond. Lights burn dimmer, smoke grows denser, the indefinite grows more and more indefinite. You wonder what would happen if a broken rail should send your train off that line of arches which overstretches London— the highway of the age of mechanism bringing you into the capital and working centre of the modern mechanical system; and while you wonder still, your train flashes out as into mid-air, and you see on both sides a grey and hazy tide, twinkling with wavy lights and spanned with bridges, either vista ending in mystery. This is Father Thames; after the Tiber, greatest of rivers. Here the history of modern civilisation centres; and from Cæsar to William of Orange the possession of this water-course has been a main motive in struggles which have widened, deepened, and established human rights and wise government more than those of all other civilised countries in the same epoch. For the Thames made London, and the salt sea which ebbs and flows at its doors has kept alive liberty and prosperity through disasters which would have destroyed an inland town many times; and that municipal independence, which has never failed London, is the source of all that is healthiest and most nobly conservative in our modern political organisation.

As the river vanishes from sight, your train slows within the vast and mysterious structure, last creation of architecture, where sight and hearing are alike confounded; calls and cries, whistles and bells, a score of locomotives coming and going, trains entering and trains departing, a ceaseless flood and ebb of passengers, bewildering, confusing to every sense but their own, yet each ticketed to his destination and surely directed to his train. The system, the consummate order with which the demands of a commerce so vast are met and satisfied, the comparative quiet, the want of bustle and fussiness, impress the American more than anything else in this first impression of London. One can but recall the Romans, the great builders and organisers, the masters of all good system of civic things in the old time as these are in our day.

This is the side of English character which imposes on me, compels me to a deference and respect which deepen as I know the more of it. In taste, they are barbarians; in the application of the principles of political or social science they are *arriérés* and too tenaciously conservative; but they build better than they know, by an intuition; and the gravitation of the national character is, in spite of their prejudices against progress, carrying them to the best and safest form of civilisation—that based on an inborn morality, love of justice, and respect for human rights. It seems strange, looking at the history of England—at her imperial policy of to-day, at such huge violations of both justice and human rights as are involved in her church system, at her rule in India, at her arbitrary and, at times, wicked domineering over weak and disorganised nations—to talk of love of both justice and human rights as traits of

English character. But no man can live in London long and not understand the problem. The acts which in his government the Englishman consents to, in his individual capacity he abhors; and while his fleets beat down the unoffending gates of China and his armies commit huge fillibusterings in India, there is no great city in the world where a stranger is so certain of justice, or the weak are so effectually upheld against the strong, as in London. The law is blind, crooked, and perverse, but sure and equal; its administration is on the practice of bygone ages, slow, reticular, complicated; but where it is a question of justice, no human jurisprudence is more effective or impartial. It is too much a city of shopkeepers—but of great shopkeepers, with a large mercantile morality such as accounts for a commercial power and prosperity unrivalled since the world began.* What London does, it does slowly but well. English civilisation is not full of fine-spun theories and declamatory recognitions, but is, in all the personal relations, profoundly moral, and (if sometimes mistakenly) religious as well; and if the morality be of a rather uncharitable type, and the religion brings out now and then its Juggernaut car, it is at least something that it maintains the steady pursuit of human well-being.

All that is hard and unsympathetic, ugly and

* The little London shopkeepers cheat you with the readiness of their Italian colleagues, but the big traders know the value of commercial morality as it is understood in no other nation.

unsentimental, in London, you see as you drive or walk from the station to your hotel; all that is servile and snobbish, and respectable and extortionate, after you have got there; and as you sit by your window in the dim November evening, waiting for your coal fire to break the chill which begins to enter your soul, I misdoubt much if you do not begin to forswear England.

All that man has done for London has been to the eye ill done; nature has been bounteous to her as to few cities. Illimitable liberty of growth, equal facility of access, a plain country round, and the sea at its gates; the railway radiating and the tide ebbing and flowing with the traffic sustained by the wealth accumulated in centuries. No one knows how rich she is, and no one who has not wandered about her for weeks can conjecture how huge. We may talk of our western empire and our admirable ports, of our growth and our growing wealth; but here is, and will remain for generations, the centre of the commercial and political world, the focus of intellectual activity, and the mint of thought. Here ferments the largest and most highly-developed humanity which as yet the universal mother has given birth to, and here the whole world's intellect comes to pay its homage. We boast, but out of this mint of London comes most of what is newest as well as of what is rarest in human work. "Solitude is the nurse of all great thought," but society is its mother; and, in London, society is more complex and solitude more easy of access than in any other of all the aggregations of men. The seclusion of the backwoods is not more complete, so far as intellectual or social influences are concerned, than lodgings in some of the out-of-the-way quarters of London. The extremes meet — the publicity of the court journal and a privacy which defies the detective police; a wealth, not of individuals, as with us, but of classes, which suspends the laws of political economy, and a concomitant poverty which threatens one day to subvert them; vortices of prosperity and misery, into which society at its extremes rushes with accelerating and concentrating velocity; here a quarter where, in teeming filth, humanity is crowded out of existence, hour by hour, with a destitution and degradation of woe uniquely the property of London—a bottomless pit of misery, emergence from which into anything by death must be light and life; and then a region of palaces, with a luxury and profusion such as England's kings, even two hundred years ago, would have held as fabulous: whatever there is of most opposite and extreme in life or death, in power or utter impotence, in having or wanting, is here.

London is one of the few perennial sensations of this world—like the sea, a primeval forest, Sahara, or the multitude of stars, all measurable, doubtless, but in terms between which and the infinite we can no more perceive the distinction than we can from the top of St. Paul's perceive the margin of the city. You enter it not knowing exactly where, and when you leave it you do so by so fine degrees that you have not been able to say where the town ended and the country began. It draws all England to it. It pervades the realm. Even the cabmen do not know the whole of it. When you have spent months exploring it, you find some day a new quarter opening to your eyes. I believe that no one can appreciate it fully but an American thoroughly versed in English history and in the practical knowledge of his own country. To him all the historical associations have the mingled charms of novelty and antiquity; there is the delightful surprise of seeing a real and vitalised antiquity, which strikes him much like going into Barbarossa's cavern and finding the Middle Ages just waking up. In his picture gallery nothing is cheapened by common uses, and nothing lost by contradictory associations; Henry VIII.'s palace has not been forever a barber's shop, or the Strand a tide-way of shopkeeping. Familiarity breeds contempt, indeed, and no London-bred boy can have a reverence for an antiquity he saw white-washed yesterday. We come to the old scenes with an ancestral reverence for objects which are not only England's but ours—in which we have the romantic interest of historical cause without the galling burden of political effect. English associations are to us utterly delightful, and London especially a huge romance, a bazaar of the Arabian

Nights, in which at one time we encounter Cromwell, and at another Dick Whittington.

But do not imagine that you can get the characteristic impression of London by running over it. When curiosity is satisfied and such familiarity as a stranger can get is attained, it will still be reserved for some moment of a sublime quiet and removal from details to give you the key-note of its greatness. Where I used to live, in a suburb five miles from St. Paul's, when sitting by my study window, sight-lost from the city proper, I could hear the roar of the traffic, like the sea on a rocky shore —the rush of incessant trains along the iron ways, the rumble of myriads of drays along hundreds of miles of stone-paved streets (for which wood is now being in part substituted), each no more to the general symphony than the hum of a gnat to the sounds of a summer day—a volume of sound unintermitting from dawn till dark. Yet I was bowered in green trees, with cowslip and daisy-flecked fields spread out under my eyes — not a spire, not a chimney-stack of the metropolis visible; and the carols of larks and thrushes, the song of the nightingale, run through the web of sounds like gold and silver threads through a dingy fabric, with the twitter of scores of sparrows like tiny spangles thrown on at random. Out of the monotone bursts the individual roar of a nearer train, the scream of a whistle, and the roar dies away again into the sullen monody. This is audible London.

If you want to see what the traffic of London is

like, go to Clapham Junction, where the great railway systems connect. The rails lie together like the wires of a grand piano. System and organisation have done their best, and nearly two thousand trains a day run over them. It is a bewilderment. In and out, coming, going, slow trains and fast trains: one side of you halts a train, and while you watch its wheels slowing, an express rushes past on the other side like a tornado of iron; no shrieking of whistles or clanging of bells as on our railways — they keep their signals for their officials, and outsiders must expose themselves at their own risks—only a rush, a blast of wind that almost takes your breath or draws you into its eddy when it has gone by, a torrent of carriage windows, and you see the rear of the last carriage shrinking before your eyes as it leaves you; and the fast express has come and gone in a space of time which you could hardly find on the dial of your watch. Up and down the lines you see signal-posts and semaphores — arms working; by night lamps green, red, white, the language of the railway, but no confusion; every man knows his place, or forgets it at his bodily peril. You ask the official when your train is due: "In two minutes"; and as the clock hands point, the train comes. He knows to the second when it left the last station, whether it be on table-time or behind it, as it generally is; every movement is recorded, and every train has its place and moment. A tunnel-way for passengers connects the whole, so that no one is allowed to cross the rails except the officials, who grow foolhardy and now and then come to grief. The guard at the junction told me one day of the killing of one of the porters, who undertook to cross the line in front of the fast express, and was struck midway the rails by the full front of the locomotive. He was knocked like a ball twenty feet, and when they reached him there was no quiver even in his flesh. If a shot from a twenty-inch Rodman gun had hit him, it would not have expunged life more completely and instantaneously. It is a saying of the denizens about Clapham Junction, that, on the average, one man is killed every six weeks. One wonders, after having watched the traffic a half-hour, that some one is not killed every day. Look cityward and see the trains flying — diverging eastward, westward, northward, line under line three deep, crossing each other, diving under or going over, but never on the same level, and then sweeping by long curves round the huge circumference of suburban London, a girdle of iron, meeting, crossing, uniting, separating again on the opposite side.

Neither the sounds nor the sights of London impressed me as did its labyrinth of railways; no other evidence of the power and intelligence of England has ever seemed to me like this stupendous accumulation of engineering accomplishment: tunnels under the river and bridges over it; the long arcades of the railway approaches, and the still more surprising vaults of the underground tunnelling under the dense houses, with an inner circle of communication—the most surprising engineering feat in the world, and perhaps the most costly, considering its extent, the cost being £1,000,000 per mile, and all to help you get about the city quicker. If the enterprise be astonishing, how much more the need which impelled it and maintains it.

But, imperial as London is in all that pertains to industrial and commercial power, it is in the architectural manifestations of metropolitanism (except size) as provincial as New York or Boston. It is impossible to say that architectural feeling is exotic in England, not knowing with absolute certainty whether they were Englishmen who built the magnificent old cathedrals or not; but it does seem that, since the race was what it is, anything æsthetic is a chance flower, and of so rare occurrence that its exceptionality—its want of visible cause and effect in precedent or succession—proves the rule more clearly than though no example had ever been found. The cities of the civilised and half-civilised world will not furnish another such collection of hideous public edifices, with so little originality, so little sense of fitness or artistic insight, as the capital of England shows. A man who could develop artistic fire in such surroundings must be of a genius irrepressible by any compression of circumstance. St. Paul's is a squat parody on St. Peter's, with everything that is ugly of the original and no advantage of position like it— no approaches, no *ensemble*, a petrified infraction of common-sense and æsthetic judgment. The British Museum is an ill-harmonised *pot-pourri* of Greek motives; Trafalgar square, a curious antithesis to the *Place de la Concorde*, with the elaborate imitation of that freak of some barbarous Roman, "Pompey's Pillar," instead of the obelisk, and that ludicrous combination of the shut-up and elongated, the National Gallery, crowning it. Even most of the later buildings, when there is a determined effort to be original, impress the stranger as ghastly evolutions of the stuff of which nightmares are made. All things impress one with an immense sense of solidity and stolidity, and, if I am not over-fanciful, with a latent contempt of the outside as compared with the inside of the house, inherent in the English nature. What that most characteristic defect of London — its smoke — may have to do with this utter want of sympathy with the exteriors of their buildings in the minds of modern Londoners, I can only conjecture; but if the city were another Venice, it could only be kept beautiful by pouring its canals daily over its buildings.

I recall some of those dreary days of my first November, 1852, when, sitting by my hotel window in the City, I used to look out into the midday gloom under the impenetrable veil, with a shadowless world before me, and recall the oppression of this inversion of fantastic elements, where by day the air was thick and oppressive, and when night fell the stars came out with their little consolations for the loss of the greater luminary, and could see the black flakes of condensed coal-smoke come drifting, floating down like the first flakes of a snow-fall — a snow of soot, visible, palpable, disastrous to gloves and linen as to stonework and to colour in all things. And what is odd, too, this comes from the very love of brightness and cheeriness at home. Offer to the Englishman to-morrow a fuel which would heat his house without flame or smoke; give him furnaces which would consume all his fuel in some subterranean recess, like our own, and he would utterly and peremptorily refuse the boon. To him his open grate and its cheerful flame, pitchy and smoke-evolving as it is, are the roc's egg to his home. London may be dingy and smoky, Stygian in darkness and diurnal in its Egyptian curse, but *his* glad hearth shall glow while soft coal comes from the mine. It shall darken and gloom until it is a new Pompeii of drifting soot from its million chimney-volcanoes, before the individual love of light and comfort shall become civic, and London burn her own smoke!

Civilisation and Christianity are in all intermediate stages at odds; the former in the highest ferment does but disengage the latter as a volatile essence. Civilisation brings out by inexorable logic those extremes of human condition from both of which Agur prayed to be preserved. The rich grow richer and the poor poorer, and the laws of political economy go on asserting themselves, by which we see that he who has the power, has a law by which he may make it greater, and he who has it not shall lose even the little he seems to have; and as in London the energy of political economy and of progressive civilisation have found their largest expression, we must expect to find men divided into the widest extremes of social condition—wealth fabulous and poverty incredible. To one who has tried the hard side of human existence and known how little will keep a man or woman from the grave, it is enough to say that men and women die statistically in London from starvation—not the sudden death of men shut in a dungeon so to die, but with long and unrelieved deprivation just sufficient to make them waste away with intolerable craving, mocked by the merest dalliance with alimentation. Some such in their involuntary apotheosis I have seen — with their gaunt faces glued to those flaming windows of the Cheapside chop-houses, looking with hungry eyes and tremulous lips at the piles of luscious steaks and saddles of prime mutton, the hell of Tantalus without his sin, for these are mostly the honest, as honesty goes in London streets — stand with unmoving faces and unconscious of whatever goes on around them, like fascinated beings unable to break away from the charm. I remember especially a young girl, not over twelve, whose face I saw pressed against the window-pane of a restaurant where I was lunching one day—a grave, hollow-eyed creature, who, without a smile or a change of any feature save the rolling of her eyes from one dainty to another during the whole of my lunchtime, fed her only available sense on this phantom banquet — but who, when on going out I offered her a huge piece of plain cake, refused it in fright and with crimsoned cheeks, as though I had caught her in theft; and it was only after repeated insistence, and on my telling her to take it home to the little ones (for there are always little ones in this case), that she took it, bewildered, and went her way.

Spiritual gravitation is as irresistible as physical, and men fly to its centre as grains of sand to the earth; the weaker and the less individual they are, the sooner they obey the law; only the few who have the centrifugal power of self-assertion can live content away from others. The clodhopper who digs and never dreams or knows what lies beyond his farm remains rustic; but once he has come within the attraction of the aggregate humanity of the city, he drifts helpless into the vortex, and rots and dies in the mass of corrupted humanity—helpless in himself, because he had not strength to stand alone, and hopeless, because there are so many like him that no human prevision could care for all the poor of a great city like London. It is no place for the helpless and the friendless, and yet it is precisely those who drift most readily to it. There seems to be a universal belief among the very poor that help is only in great cities. Dick Whittington entertained a very common superstition and strengthened it; and Heaven only knows how many, with this golden dream in their hearts, have gone to London to die in its dirt or drown in its tide. And once in the city, the deluded never leave it; the company in misery which it offers to them is better than any emigration; the fascination of crowds is stronger, even with better men and women, than any good in solitary independence. This and the innate laziness of mankind, the insanity to escape all bonds of labour, are more the causes of the destitution and misery of London than any social wrong or want of charity and benevolence in the wealthy. These great cities will always be crowded to the last limits of their capacity. Relieve the importunate and improvident of to-day by a determinate provision, and to-morrow there will appear mysteriously as many new improvidents and unfortunates, candidates for the same provision; the whole realm of beggary and imprevision will make a hitch forward, and the serried line will still stand like that at the post-office windows or theatre doors at times, waiting for another vacancy and pushing on, always as long, always as miserable, and all the more improvident as provision is made by others. This is the poverty of London: not a chance-come misfortune which some sad widow may have in a country village, her support and provider being suddenly gone, struggling with a new and straiter living to which in time she adapts herself or dies; not a sudden cutting away of the small margin and a distress in the house for rent, which hard working sometimes gives a labourer, but an habitual living on what may come through picking up by chance — pilfering and stealth to the worse and slow starvation to the better natures, with gradual extinction of all that is human to all — squalor, filth, a sinking till sense of degradation is lost and the poor soul slides into utter vice as a boat adrift goes down into the sea.

Look into the quarters of this poverty: for convenience, in some of the streets about Goodman's Fields, swarming like ant-hills: shoals of children of all ages below four or five encumbering the road-way, careless of carriage wheels, for no vehicle ever enters here except the huckster's cart or the parish hearse; frousy, sodden, beer-soaked faces of women thrust out at the windows, cursing their brats who cry in the dirt below; sauntering men who look at you, if you are decently dressed, as if your personal safety were a wrong and injustice to them; young girls, filthy, slatternly, leering, jeering, and ogling, imagination can readily conceive what for. Men do not grow to manhood in such slums and sunless ways, or women to virtue or dignity. All is squalor and filth and utter degradation of the divine image. And this is one of the inevitable results of the highest civilisation, as certainly as that London is greatest and most civic of all great cities.

For the other great result you have not far to go. In that region of grim and forbidding palaces, which, like Ali Baba's cave, are nothing to him who has not, but everything for him who has, the "open sesame," any one will answer our purpose — this one, for instance, with a covered way from the door to the street, lest its dainty inmates should catch a drop of rain on the way to their carriage. Within all is order and decorous silence. The foot falls on deep-piled carpets. In the intonation of the low-toned command is the highest expression of that incommunicable, indescribable, and, except by generations of cultivation, unattainable quality we call *high* breeding. In the reply to it is that perfect antithesis in breeding, which we ought to call *low* — the profound, unquestioning, and unhesitating prostration of self of the traditional hereditary "servant," disciplined like a soldier, who, as his master never permits himself to express a disturbing emotion, never allows *himself* an expression of surprise or a word of comment; whose self-command is as great as his master's, perhaps greater—a well apparelled statue, save when an order is given; whose bows and deference for his master's guests are graduated by the distance at which they sit from the head of the table; a human creature that sees nothing, knows nothing, and believes nothing which his master does not expect him to see and know and believe; who, if he thinks of a heaven at all, never dreams that it can be the same thing for his master and himself: he hopes to meet his father and grandfather and great-grandfather in the servants' hall of that celestial abode where his master and all the family for countless generations will dwell in their mundane state; his brains could no more take in the parable of Dives and Lazarus than the laws of Kepler, and the most insensate Chartist or Radical could never inspire in him an ambition to be anything beyond butler in his master's mansion.

All the gorgeousness and luxury about them —master and servant—are the fit trappings of the gentleman's estate. They two make one, a kind of social centaur, a single brain and a double body. The civic mechanism necessitates other grades of mankind, but this is the summit level. The centaur may be the highest expression of human culture; he may be a mere vehicle of pleasures—betting, horse-racing, with no conception of or respect for that culture. He is to all the world the personation of human dignity, and the King or Queen is only the head of his order. He may enjoy the refinements his ancestors' wealth has gathered round him, and justify his position, or he may bury himself deeper in stultifying indulgences by the weight of it—be the best or worst of men; he is still the cynosure of the Old World's regards—*milord Anglais*. In his sphere the echo of social wants and wrongs dies away; the tenants on his estate are as well cared for as his favourite flocks, and he does his duty to all who depend socially on him. Beyond, all is ignored which disturbs the serenity of that earthly heaven in whose immobility he abides. For his existence, civilisation, law, order, the church, army, and navy are the guaranties and pre-requisites. It is for him, according to the original theory of the British constitution, that the state exists.

In other European countries of approximate civilisation, his congener has gone under; he, wiser, draws up to him the social elements that might menace his supremacy, and which, by their necessity to the state, are necessary to him— the banker, the successful administrator, soldier, admiral, and even the church, whose power is not of this world, is led in by its lord bishops. So that the centaur, being the governing and the governed in one, wins over from any possible opposition, whatever elements may be assimilated to his class, which outside its limits might be dangerous, and so fights off the fate which has befallen his congeners of the Continent.

In the strictest social creed of the centaur, it is held as an essential to this assimilation that the candidate shall not only never have done anything useful for its due compensation, but that society shall not be able to remember when one of his ancestors did so, the bluest blood being that of him whose remote forefather did but follow the original centaurial proposition of taking all that they wanted wherever they found it, and, by levying contributions on all the classes of society, enabling his remotest heirs and successors to enjoy the proceeds in complete and reputable abstention from gain by any useful employment — useless labour, such as breeding and running race-horses, etc., or unpaid labour in science and art being perfectly allowable and possibly praiseworthy, with centaurial honours.

Although socially dominant in all England, the centaur is only to be known in London in perfection, or the extent of his dominance to be recognised. He must have his residence in London, no matter how many others he may have, and it must be worthy his position. There are here and there certain literary and intellectual heresies and heretics refusing to recognise centaurdom as the highest of human good; but, in general, the people accept the distinction by which, when they are overridden by the centaurs, they are privileged to override some one else in the grade below them, and each one in the long file of social gradation is permitted and perhaps expected to be a toady to the superior, and a bully to the inferior grades. And down to the very substratum of beggars and crossing-sweepers, there is a keen recognition of the social stamp of "useless" and "useful," and an inherent contempt of the latter individual as such. I have noticed scores of times that, when I was carrying a package through the streets of London, the beggars and sweepers paid no attention to me. The centaur and the beggar agree in one thing, that a man who carries his own parcels is beneath their social recognition.

It is to London, as the centre of all that England is or can be, that these two classes gravitate—the poles of civilised humanity; nowhere but in London could they find their commensurate importance, and here they attain their highest perfection and greatest development. Beggary and aristocracy are the productions *par excellence* of the metropolis of civilisation; the traits which, even more than its size and wealth, distinguish it from all the cities of the earth.

And from all this antagonism of extremes, from all the heat and ferment of this alembic of humanity—there comes not only much refuse—dead matter which goes back to decay and first disorganisation—but there distils the truest, divinest spirit humanity can embody. Here does but disengage more quickly and more perfectly, what may be of better than aristocracy and more beautiful than court or state. If the individual is securest in his individuality, if the one talent is best buried in the retirement of rustic life, if philosopher and poet find in their hearts to say with their Roman confrère, "*Procul, procul este profana*," and float tranquilly down the stream of life alone, yet in the thickest mêlée is the most strength won; and in spite of the terrible perversion of Christianity, and the palsying condition of social organisation, one can find here the rarest types of Christian and of mankind. Who escapes humanity shuns God.

I am not a lover of great cities; their ambitions and ideals, their vulgarities and their urbanities, are alike distasteful to me; but I must say that I have known in London the most angelic natures that it has ever been in my lot to encounter. Perhaps I should have seen still better if my eyes had been open wider.

And it is in this very class which I have, in no disparaging sense, termed centauric, the aristocracy, where social independence has reached its highest, that we find here and there, cased like the flower and fruit of this mighty growth, in extraneous and deciduous leafage, that best type of humanity as the world knows it, the true English gentlefolk—beings whose exterior decorum may be counterfeited by an emulator, whose inmost gentleness and courtesy may be shadowed forth in peer or peasant who love their kind, and feel the common bond of divine birth; but whose most perfect expression of noble demeanour and large-heartedness can only be found where the best type of mind has been permitted the largest and richest culture and the completest freedom of hereditary development in the most favourable external circumstances. There are nobles and noblemen—men who seem to be conscious only that surrounding men are lower than they; and others whose illumination pervades every one near them and brings all up into the same world of light and sweetness. The prestige of nobility is founded on a true human instinct; occasionally one finds an English nobleman who justifies its existence, and makes us snobs in spite of our democracy.

I could, I am certain, point to Americans who, in every substantial trait of the gentleman, will stand comparison with any aristocrat born—men in whom gentlehood has grown to hereditary ripeness; the third and fourth generations of men who have cultivated on American soil the virtues of honesty, morality, sincerity, courtesy, self-abnegation, humanity, benevolence; men and women whose babyhood was cradled in those influences which make what we call "good breeding," and to whom the various vulgarities of our parvenu princes are as foreign as to the bluest-blooded heir of Norman fortune; and this is to me a more grateful and sympathetic type of humanity than that of its English congener. But to this will always be lacking one grace which that may possess — the majesty of the born legislator and ruler; the air of habitual command and control, hereditary as are all generic traits, good or bad, and which imposes itself on the consciousness of all men. This, be it for the bettering or the worsering of the type, is to our democratic, ruled, levelled, and ballot-boxed civilisation forbidden forever; and the fustian heredities of quickly and perhaps ill-made millionaires, for ever so many times told, will never be other than a curious caricature of it. Theoretically, we must gainsay it; but when all is said, be it of our original paradise-planting, or a devil's graft got among the thorns and thistles of our exile, the growth of a certain reverence for a time-honoured nobility has become a part of every gentle nature, which only time and assiduity can, but which they certainly will eradicate—but not to-day, nor while the English nobility is what, as a whole, it is. We may prefer, in our struggles of race, the independence of the Athenian hoplite, of the quick-footed runner; but the centaur had his side of the story, and the same marble immortalises them both.

We Americans are fond of talking of being our own masters; but the man who is his own master is also his own servant. A well-disciplined army is the type of highest human development — compassionate, unflinching strategy in its head; intelligent, unhesitating and unquestioning obedience in its body. He who in an army will exercise his own judgment and will, is a mutineer. Independence means isolation and incompletion; association is the true life, social, political, and spiritual.

The empire of England owes its existence to this phenomenon. The brain to command coupled with the nerve to obey, and both to care less for annihilation than for defeat; the will to lead and the will to follow, co-ordination as if of brain and hand; the union of antitheses in an existence more effective and powerful, socially and politically, than the most perfect individuality—that is what I mean by the centaur, a higher evolution of civic life than our boasted political equality and personal independence. This makes empire possible and reconcilable with the good of ruler and ruled alike. And more than this, it is the greatest element in that cause which has for effect that, while every other wealthy nation in our time is drifting into a social conflict of ominous outlook, with growing political and social corruption, England has steadily risen in civic and political purity. Wherever else I look, in Europe, at least, I see only reform by revolution, while in England it comes steadily by law.

London is indeed a microcosm, not merely that it is large, but because everything is in it; and with all its intense commonplaceness and humdrum conservatism, there is a degree of unexpectedness which keeps one on an intellectual alert. No city grows like it; yet you pass from quarters of new palaces, on ground which even I remember as once an expanse of kitchen-gardens as remote from metropolitanism as the hop-fields of Kent, to others where the dinginess of the Middle Ages seems to linger, and where the only change of the century past must be of deaths and births; into "no thoroughfare" squares, round which the flood of improvement has swept without entering; into places that impress one with the idea of antiquity far more than does the Parthenon or the Colosseum, dusty, grassy, and silent, where, if you chance to see a merry, playing child, it startles you as an anachronism. One day, perhaps, the republic and the proletary and the boulevard will come: be sure that they will be to the breaking of many hearts grown old in a world of circumstance and association which will not suffer change.

But, to the mere passenger, London's most

attractive point is her suburban wealth — the lovely wedding of city and country in Richmond, Twickenham, and Barnes, and so all round by Clapham, Dulwich, Norwood, and the Crystal Palace, but especially near the Thames, whose lovely windings, with frequent villages and luxuriant meadows always green with that vivid greenness which no climate besides this can boast of, remind me of the early-summer Mohawk in its most gentle portions. Great glades of oak and elm come down to the water's edge, and a sward that all the year round is like a carpet, with a river-fringe of willows and flags, and the swans going in and out undisturbed, following the ebb down to the city even, and the flood back to their homes, running the gauntlet of steamer and wherry, with none to make them afraid; and the lazy, picturesque barges drift down from their inland markets, catching the ebb while it serves, and waiting at anchor till it comes again, their rusty tackle and tawny sails so unlike what our seafaring man would settle his fancy to, and yet so beloved by painters and etchers.

Yes, London ends as it began, with the Thames. The dreamy reaches of its upper course, with their framing of rural picturesqueness, their wealth of park and villa, the meed and stimulus at once of the greatest of commercial communities, run by insensible degrees of change into those so unlike in all surroundings, so stirring and vibrant with commerce and speculation; and the two extremes, corresponding as heart and brain the one to the other, or as root and branch, are what makes the life and immensity of London, and, in one sense, of England. Above the river in which the miserable perish and on which the fortunate grow rich, runs the other tide whose flood leads on to fortune, whose sources are in the sea empire, and which debouches in the lands of the little island; above the river of the painters and poets, winding through the downs and meadows of the rarest of cultivated landscape out to the reaches where the melancholy sea breeds its fogs and damp east winds, is that of the merchant and politician, having its springs in the uttermost parts of the earth, and pouring out its golden tribute on the lands whence the other steals its drift and ooze. Ill dawns the day for humanity when England's prosperity finds its final flood.

JOHN RUSKIN

I

I WAS sitting one afternoon with Longfellow, on the porch of the old house at Cambridge, when the conversation turned on intellectual development, and he referred to a curious phenomenon, of which he instanced several cases, and which he compared to the double stars, of two minds not personally related but forming a binary system, revolving simultaneously around each other and around some principle which they regarded in different lights. I do not remember his instances, but that which at once came to my mind was the very interesting one of Turner and Ruskin. The complementary relation of the great writer and the imaginative painter is one of the most—indeed, the most interesting that I know in intellectual history: the one a master in all that belongs to verbal expression but singularly deficient in the gifts of the artist, feeble in drawing, with a most inaccurate perception of colour and no power of invention; the other the most stupendous of idealists, the most consummate master of colour orchestration the world has ever seen, but so curiously devoid of the gifts of language that he could hardly learn to write grammatically or coherently, and when he spoke, omitting so many words that often his utterances, like those of a child, required interpretation by one accustomed to his ways before a stranger could understand them. Ruskin is a man reared and moulded in the straightest Puritanism, abhorring uncleanness of all kinds, generous to extravagance, moved by the noblest humanitarian impulses, morbidly averse to anything that partakes of sensuality, and responsive as a young girl to appeals to his tenderness and compassion. Turner was a miser; churlish; a satyr in his morals—not merely a sensualist, but satisfied only by occasional indulgences in the most degrading debauchery; and even in his painting sometimes giving expression to images so filthy that when, after his death, the trustees came to overhaul his sketches, there were many which they were obliged to destroy in regard for common decency. It is hardly possible to conceive of a more complete antithesis than that in the natures of these two, who turn, and will turn so long as English art and English letters endure, around the same centre of art and each around the other. In fact, to the great majority of our race Turner is seen through the eyes of Ruskin, and Ruskin is only known as the eulogist of Turner.

The conjunction leaves both misunderstood by the general mind. Ruskin looks at the works of the great landscape painter much as the latter looked at nature—not for what is in the thing looked at, but for the sentiments it awakens. The world's art does not present anything to rival Turner's in its defiance of nature. He used nature when it pleased him to do so, but when it pleased him better he belied her with the most reckless audacity. He had absolutely no respect for truth. His colour was the most splendid of impossibilities, and his topography like the geography of dreams; yet Ruskin has spent a great deal of his life in persuading himself and the world that that colour was scientifically correct, and in hunting for the points of view from which he drew his compositions. His conviction that Turner was always doing his best, if in a mysterious way, to tell the truth about nature is invincible. Early in the period of my acquaintance with him we had a vivacious discussion on this matter in his own house; and to convince him that Turner was quite indifferent as to matters of natural phenomena, I called Ruskin's attention to the view out of the window, which was of the Surrey hills, a rolling country whose grassy heights were basking in a glorious summer sunlight and backed by a pure blue sky, requesting him then to have brought down from the room where it was hung a drawing by Turner in which a similar effect was treated. The hill in nature was, as it always will be if covered by vegetation and under the same circumstances, distinctly darker than the sky; Turner's was relieved in pale yellow green against a deep blue sky, stippled down to a delicious aërial profundity. Ruskin gave up the case in point, but still clung to the general rule. In fact, having begun his system of art teaching on the hypothesis that Turner's way of seeing nature was scientifically the most correct that art knew, he had never been able to abandon it and admit that Turner only sought, as was the case, chromatic relations which had no more to do with facts of colour than the music of Mendelssohn's "Wedding March" has to do with the emotions of the occasion on which it is played. His assumption of Turner's veracity is the corner-stone of his system, and its rejection would be the demolition of that system.

His art criticism is radically and irretrievably wrong. That which makes art what it is, *as art*, has absolutely nothing to do with the phenomena of nature. Even limiting the term *Art* to that form of it embraced in Design, this is true. The end of art, *as art*, is decoration; and the earliest, as well as some of the most exquisite decoration we know of, is in combination of forms and colours which are not borrowed from nature. Some of the best art in the world is devoted to the invention of purely conventional forms for purely decorative purposes, and in decorative work any attempt at distinct naturalism is at once felt as degrading the decoration. One day that Ruskin and myself were discussing the theory of art, he asked me to formulate one. I complied, with this, "Art is the harmonic (rhythmic or melodic) expression of human emotion." He expressed himself so pleased with it that he asked permission to give it in a note to one of the later volumes of "Modern Painters," which he was then passing through the press. It never appeared. On second thought, he doubtless perceived that it clashed with the expressions he had employed in the work. Art does not lie in representing nature, but in the manner of representing her, and may equally be employed in invented and conventional forms, as in repeating hers. Naturalism and art are the eternal antithesis —as one rises the other sinks in the scale of the general results. No art can be gauged by its fidelity to nature unless we admit in that term the wider sense which makes nature of the human soul and all that is—the sense of music, the perception of beauty, the grasp of imagination, "the light that never was, on sea or land," as well as that which serves the lens of the photographer; and Ruskin's own work, his teaching in his classes, and his application of his own standards to all great work, show that he understands the term "fidelity to nature" to mean the adherence to physical facts, the scientific aspects of nature. Greek art he never has really sympathised with, nor at heart accepted as supreme, though years after he took the position he never has avowedly abandoned, he found that in Greek coinage there were artistic qualities of the highest refinement; but Watts has told me that Ruskin expressed his surprise that the artist could keep before him so ugly a thing as the Oxford Venus, a cast of which was in his studio, and that he pronounced the horse an animal devoid of all beauty. In my opinion, he cares nothing for the plastic qualities of art, or for the human figure, otherwise than as it embodies human and moral dignity. The diverse and incongruous criticisms he makes on Titian, Michael Angelo, and Raphael, put side by side with his notes on Holman Hunt, on George. Leslie and Miss Thompson in the Royal Academy, and Miss Alexander's drawings, show his appreciation of figure art to be absolutely without any criterion of style or motive in figure painting, if this were not already apparent from his contradictions at different periods of his life. These are puzzling to the casual reader. When he says, in the early part of "Modern Painters," that the work of Michael Angelo in general, the *Madonna di San Sisto*, and some other works are at the height of human excellence, and later demolishes poor Buonarotti like a bad plaster cast, and sets Raphael down as a mere posturer and dexterous academician, one is at a loss to reconcile his opinions with any standard. The fact, I believe to be, that his early art education, which was in great part due to J. D. Harding, a painter of high executive powers and keen appreciation of technical abilities in the Italian painters, was in the vein of orthodox standards; that while under the influence of his reverence for his teachers he accepted the judgment which they, in common with most artists, have passed on the old masters; but that when left to himself, with no kind of sympathy with ideal figure art, nor, I believe, with any form of figure art as such, but with a passion for landscape, a curious enthusiasm for what is minute and intense in execution, and an over-weening estimate of his own standards and opinions, he gradually lost all this vicarious appreciation, and retained of his admiration of old art only what was in accordance with his own feelings—*i.e.*, the intensity of moral and religious fervour, and, above all, anything that savoured of mysticism, the ascetic and didactic, especially the art of the schools of religious passion. This was due to the profound devotional feeling which was the basis of his intellectual nature. He said to me once that he was a long time in doubt whether he should give himself to the church or to art. So far as the world is concerned I think he took the wrong road. In the church he might not have been, as his father hoped, a bishop, for his views have been too individual for church discipline, but I believe he would have produced a more beneficial effect on his age than if he had been. As an art critic he has been like one writing on the sea-sands: his system and his doctrines of art are repudiated by every thoughtful artist I know. Art in certain forms touches him profoundly but only emotionally. Although he drew earnestly for years, he never seemed to understand style in drawing, master as he is of style (*sui generis*) in language; his perception of colour is so deficient that he appears to me unable to recognise the true optical colour of any object; that is, its colour in sunshine as distinguished from its colour in shadow or its local colour; and in painting from nature he is always best pleased with what is most like Turner. I painted or sketched with him during a summer in

Switzerland, and therefore I do not speak from a moral consciousness. What he most admired in my work, and sought in his own, was excessive elaboration and photographic fidelity, and he did not easily apprehend the larger relations of the landscape. He used to wonder at my getting over the detail so fast; but he always got angry with the work when I reached a point where I found it necessary to bring the masses into relation according to my own ideas. At Chamonix I one day began a large study of the Mer de Glace from opposite the glacier, looking up it with the Aiguille de Dru in the centre of the distance. The whole subject was rapidly laid in in general effect until it got down to the foreground, where I began finishing elaborately, to his entire satisfaction, which continued for several days, and until I pointed out to him a difficulty which it puzzled me to get over without violating the topographical fidelity of the study. There were several of the main lines of the distance which formed approximately radii from a point of no importance in the composition. He had not noticed it; but when I pointed it out he got into a state of vexation, and, declaring that nothing could be done with a subject which had such an awkward accident in it, insisted on my giving up the study, saying he would not stay in Chamonix for me to finish it. As I was his guest I complied with his wish, and we left the valley the next day.

This capriciousness is a characteristic of the man. In spite of the womanly tenderness of his nature, which is, when favourably moved, of a kindliness which measures no sacrifice, he is capable, under impulse, of treating a friend of one day with the most contemptuous aversion on the next, for some whim no more important than that which drove us out of Chamonix.

There is in his character a curious form of individuality, so accentuated and so imperious that it produces in him the sense of his own infallibility. He once wrote of his opinions as not matters of opinion but as positive knowledge; yet, in personal intercourse, one finds nothing of the dogmatism which is so notable a feature in his writing. He listened to all objections, and often acknowledged, during discussion, the inconsequence of his conclusions; and during the long and vigorous debates which occupied our Swiss evenings, he not infrequently admitted error, but on the next day held the old ground as firmly as ever. His intellect, with all its power and intensity, is of the purely feminine type. The love of purity; the quick, kindly, and unreasoning impulse; the uncompromising self-sacrifice when the feeling is on him, and the illogical self-assertion in reaction when it has passed; the passionate admiration of power; the waywardness and often inexplicable fickleness—all are there. But behind all these feminine traits there is the no less feminine quality of passionate love of justice, flecked, on occasions of personal implication, with acts of great injustice; there is a general inexhaustible tenderness, with occasional instances of absolute cruelty. Any present judgment of him, as a whole, is difficult if not impossible, because there are in him several different individuals, and the perspective in which we now see them, makes of his position, as an art teacher, the most prominent element of his personality; whereas, in my persuasion, his art teaching is, in his own nature and work, subordinate to his moral and humanitarian ideals. He always saw art through a religious medium, and this made him, from the beginning, strain his system of teaching and criticism to meet the demand of direct truth to nature, the roots of his enthusiasm and reverence being not in art but in nature, and in her beneficial influence on humanity.

A little incident of our Alpine summer will illustrate this view of his character better than all my appreciations. During our stay at Geneva he had some mountain drawing to do at the Perte du Rhône, and asked me to drive down with him. Not far from the point of view which he had selected was a group of wretched dwellings, miscalled cottages, but which in America they call shanties; not the picturesque wall-and-thatch structures which the word cottage calls up in England, but built of boards, shabby without being picturesque, and, to my American notions, only capable of association with poverty and discomfort. Ruskin asked me to draw them while he was drawing the mountains. The subject was anything but attractive or pictorial, and though it should have been enough for me that he wished me to draw it carefully, I only obeyed my own feeling and made a careless ten minutes' pencil drawing, all the thing was worth to me. When Ruskin drove up to take me in on the way back to Geneva and saw what I had done, he was—and, I must say, with good reason—offended at the indifferent way in which I had complied with his request, and, after a few reproachful words, threw himself back in the carriage in a sullen temper. I replied that the subject did not interest me, and that the principal feeling I had in looking at it was that it must be a wretched home for human beings, and promised more fevers than anything else; and that, in short, I did not think it worth drawing. Nothing more was said by either of us until we had driven half-way back to Geneva, when he broke out with, "You are right, Stillman, about those cottages; your way of looking at them was nobler than mine, and now, for the first time in my life, I understand how anybody can live in America." It has always seemed to me that this was a true epitome of the man's nature—first, the æsthetic outside view of the matter, then the humanitarian, overpowering it; the womanish pettishness, and the generous admission of his error when seen; and, after this confession, his greater cordiality to me — for he always valued more any one who brought him a new idea, though he often broke friendship with those who differed from him too strongly.

Besides this absorbing passion for the spiritual ideal, the mental constitution whose compass was set to the immovable pole of the most exalted morality, he had a curious facility for seeing art as he wished to. He saw through his feelings and prepossessions, and even looking at nature he only saw certain things, and those in general through his predisposition. So he always held Turner true although the thing he saw was false. In one drawing, where Turner has given the full moon rising in cool night-mists at the left of the picture and the sun setting golden at the right, Ruskin explains it as intended to be two pictures. He praises Turner for mingled effects of sunlight and moonlight when he ought to know that the full moon will cast no shadow until the sun has set nearly or quite an hour. Turner continually puts figures in full light in the foreground of a picture which has the sun setting in the view, the shadows on the figures being consequently on the side nearest the sun, yet Ruskin has never admitted the painter's indifference to the facts of nature.

II

To the world at large Ruskin's reputation, even as an art critic, rests on the first volume of his "Modern Painters." Very few people have read the second volume, and fewer still the whole five, though the early editions have been sold and others since. Of this first volume, what most impressed the general public was not the soundness of his views of art, of which it could not judge at all, or his knowledge of nature, of which it could judge but little, but his eloquence, his magnificent diction. Take, for instance, the following from the comparison of Turner with Poussin, which every reader of the book will remember as what is called a "word picture" of extraordinary power:

"But as I climbed the long slopes of the Alban mount, the storm swept finally to the north, and the noble outline of the domes of Albano, and the graceful darkness of its ilex grove rose against pure streaks of alternate blue and amber, the upper sky gradually flushing through the last fragments of rain-cloud in deep, palpitating azure, half ether and half dew. The noonday sun came slanting down the rocky slopes of La Riccia, and its masses of entangled and tall foliage, whose autumnal tints were mixed with the wet verdure of a thousand evergreens, were penetrated with it as with rain. I cannot call it colour, it was conflagration. *Purple, and crimson, and scarlet, like the curtains of God's tabernacle, the rejoicing trees sank into the valley in showers of light, every separate leaf quivering with bouyant and burning life, each, as it turned to reflect or to transmit the sunbeam, first a torch and then an emerald.* Far up into the recesses of the valley, the green vistas arched like the hollows of mighty waves of some crystalline sea, *with the arbutus flowers dashed along their flanks for foam, and silver flakes of orange spray tossed into the air around them, breaking over the gray walls of rock into a thousand separate stars, fading and kindling alternately as the weak wind lifted or let them fall.* Every glade of grass burned like the golden floor of heaven, opening in sudden gleams as the foliage broke and closed above it *as sheet lightning opens in a cloud at sunset; the motionless masses of dark rock—dark though flushed with scarlet lichen—casting their quiet shadows across its restless radiance,* the fountain underneath them filling its marble hollow with blue mist and fitful sound, and, over all, the multitudinous bars of amber and rose, the sacred clouds that have no darkness, and only exist to illumine, were seen in fathomless intervals, between the solemn and orbed repose of the stone pines passing to lose themselves in the last white, blinding lustre of the measureless line, where the Campagna melted into the blaze of the sea."

Magnificent this is as rhetoric, but, if intended to show the shortcomings of Poussin or the attainments of Turner, it is as exaggerated for one as it is unfair for the other; for the effects there described are no more in the power of colour than in the feeling of either of those artists. It is not nature-painting at all; neither true to the sense nor to the details of nature. As mastery of the English language I shall not attempt to criticise it, but as statement of what is to be seen in nature or rendered in art it bears about the same relation to the most ideal and orchestral effects of Turner as those do to sober nature. I have put in italics certain expressions to which I ask the grave critical attention of the reader. I leave out, for the moment, the singular topographical inaccuracies which, in a work devoted to truth of nature, ought to claim some attention; but, in such a work, we may ask the sober meaning of such expressions as "Purple, and crimson, and scarlet, like the curtains of God's tabernacle"; "Every separate leaf quivering with buoyant and burning life, each, as it turned to reflect or to transmit the sunbeam, first a torch and then an emerald"; the rocks "dark though flushed with scarlet lichen—casting their quiet shadows across its restless radiance" [why restless radiance, except, like much else in the passage, for alliteration?]. The colour epithets, to an artist, only express a crudity of pigment as unlike Turner as nature; the "arbutus flowers dashed along their flanks" . . . "silver flakes of orange spray [dreamed of from some other locality, for neither exists at Aricia] tossed into the air around them . . . into a thousand separate stars"; and "every separate leaf," show as great contempt for the possibilities of painting in the rendering of detail for the human eye as indifference to the aims of landscape painting, either according to Poussin or Turner. The "Purple, and crimson, and scarlet, like the curtains of God's tabernacle," is apocalyptic, not naturalistic, and the entire passage, when we consider that it is part of an essay intended to advocate the close adherence to the facts of nature in landscape painting, can only be put aside as passing legitimate criticism or justifiable comparison. It is safe to say that, of a thousand landscape painters and amateurs habituated to look at nature, taking the best and the most trivial, not one who had passed by Aricia would recognise as fact a single characteristic of the description by Ruskin. I know the place better than I do London or New York, and am confident in saying that neither in the *ensemble* nor in the detail is there anything there which Ruskin imagines he saw. Much is mere sound, alliteration which is in place in poetry but not in art criticism, and much only the expression of vague imaginings far less like nature than the great scenic compositions of John Martin.

Take another instance from the section on the sea ("Truth of Water," this being the description of a picture, the *Slave Ship*). Again I italicise the passages to which I wish to call attention as demanding analysis and criticism.

"It is a sunset on the Atlantic after prolonged storm; but the storm is partially lulled, and the torn and streaming rain-clouds *are moving in scarlet lines to lose themselves in the hollow of the night.* The whole surface of the sea included in the picture is divided into two ridges of enormous swell, not high nor local, but a broad heaving of the whole ocean like the lifting of its bosom by deep-drawn breath after the torture of the storm. Between these two ridges the fire of the sunset falls along the trough of the sea, dyeing it with an awful but glorious light, *the intense and lurid splendour of which burns like gold and bathes like blood.* . . . *Purple and blue the lurid shadows of the hollow breakers are cast on the mist of the night, which gathers cold and low, advancing like the shadow of death* upon the guilty ship as it labours amidst the lightning of the sea, its thin masts written upon the sky in lines of blood girded with *condemnation in that fearful hue which signs the sky with horror, and mixes its flaming flood with the sunlight, and, cast far along the desolate heave of the sepulchral waves, incarnadines the multitudinous sea.* I believe, if I were reduced to rest Turner's claim to immortality upon any single work, I should choose this. Its daring conception—ideal in the highest sense of the word—is fused on the purest truth and wrought out with the concentrated knowledge of a life . . . and the whole picture is dedicated to the most sublime of subjects and impressions—(completing thus the perfect system of all truth which we have shown to be formed by Turner's works)—the power, majesty, and deathfulness of the open, deep, illimitable sea."

"Burns like gold and bathes like blood" is, of course, again for alliteration; "Purple and blue the lurid shadows," etc., part for the sing of the sentence and part poetic imagination utterly unsuggested and unsuggestable by painting; "that fearful hue," etc., to "multitudinous sea," is simply fine writing which, when it conveys a false impression, or no impression legitimate to its professed purpose, is a literary vice, as it is in this case, where the purpose is the *description of a picture*.

Ruskin supposes this picture to be an attempt to pourtray the deep sea, but neither he nor Turner was ever out of soundings: how should one paint, or the other recognise, the fathomless as distinguished from the shallow seas? The fact is, that the sea in the *Slave Ship* is a long groundswell, resembling the watery mountains one may see on the open Atlantic no more than the water below a rapid. This form of swell and the "hollow breakers" are never found except when the sea is shoaling. In the deep Atlantic, after a long gale, such as Ruskin supposes (I have seen it at its worst once only in 70,000 miles, more or less, of ocean travel by sail and steam), the great waves lift to heights such that Turner's *Slave Ship* would be hidden between two of them. They hang over you like impending doom; and, just when you think that the ship must be buried in five seconds, the forefoot of the wave reaches you, and the ship suddenly begins to rise, and in another five seconds you are on the summit looking out over the heaving expanse — black, save as it is foam-driven, fitfully rising and falling, apparently without law or order — and, after being poised an instant, you feel the ship going from under you again; your breath almost leaves you with the rapidity of the descent, and you are buried once more in the deep trough of the sea for another brief space. Out of the flanks of these great waves jump and start, fitfully and unaccountably, lesser hillocks, to drop and disappear again; but, when the crest of one comes towards you, you see no hollow breaker, for the crest simply pitches forward and slides down the slope—there is no combing.

Then, as to truth, Turner's whole picture is a flagrant falsehood. The most gorgeous colours of a sunset are in it painted in a sky where the sun has still half an hour or more to sink to the horizon; and this license the artist habitually took, although, as every artist knows, these colours never come till after the sun is below the horizon. A suggestion of them is given by a winter sunset in the smoke of London, but there is not the least suggestion of the chromatic scale Turner uses. Lowell used to say that Turner learned to paint sunsets in London; but the London smoke sunset is a display in tonality more like Cuyp than Turner, sometimes gorgeous but never brilliant colour. Cuyp was a tonalist, Turner a colourist, and Turner in the *Slave Ship* reached the highest attainment I know in colour orchestration. The picture is in a flame of sunset colours; but, in the lower left-hand corner, is a bit of blue and white, the American flag, which, like the blare of a trumpet in a florid passage of music, throws the whole scheme into a startling contrast. The clouds are not the " torn and streaming rain-clouds" of an afterstorm sky, but full-bellied, rolling wind-clouds, so far as they are structurally true to anything; subtly modelled and modulated, but, as a whole, as utterly impossible a sky as the sea is an utterly impossible sea. It is a marvellous picture: I do not yield to Ruskin in admiration of it as art, or admire it less for its daring license and contempt of nature's details; one can only say that it is magnificent, but it is not nature. Ruskin's feeling as to art may have been, *au fond*, correct; but it was so disturbed and perverted by his theories and the settled conviction that art was simply the uncompromising rendering of nature as she appears to the bodily vision, that he left out of all consideration the subjective* transformation of natural truth which is the basis of art; or, if he reckoned it in, it was to persuade himself that it was due to a peculiarity of vision in the painter. It is impossible to reconcile all the inconsistencies into which this theory led him; such as the exaltation of painters who were mere naturalists, like Brett, or utterly unimaginative realists, like Holman Hunt, and the extraordinary judgment which he pronounced

---

* I remember that he used to express the strongest abhorrence of the terms "subjective" and "objective" as German nonsense.

on Millais in his pamphlet on Pre-Raphaelitism —which phase of art he desired to consider the consequence of his teaching, though, as I have heard Rossetti say, none of the Brotherhood had ever read ten pages of his writing before Ruskin had constituted himself their advocate. In some respects this little book may be considered the summing up of his art teachings, and the violence done to logic and art alike in his parallel between Millais and Turner is the clearest statements of his errors we possess. The function of the painter is here defined clearly and chiefly to be *topographer and historian.*

"Suppose that, after disciplining themselves so as to be able to draw with unerring precision each the particular kind of subject in which he most delighted, they had separated into two great armies of historians and naturalists; that the first had painted with absolute faithfulness every edifice, every city, every battle-field, every scene of the slightest historical interest, precisely and completely rendering their aspect at the time; and that their companions, according to their several powers, had painted with like fidelity the plants and animals, the natural scenery and the atmospherical phenomena of every country on the earth; suppose that a faithful and complete record were now in our museums of every building destroyed by war, or time, or innovation during these last 200 years; suppose that each recess of every mountain chain of Europe had been penetrated and its rocks drawn with such accuracy that the geologist's diagram was no longer necessary; suppose that every tree of the forest had been drawn in its noblest aspect, every beast of the field in its savage life—that all these gatherings were already in our national galleries, and that the painters of the present day were labouring happily and earnestly to multiply them and put such knowledge more and more within reach of the common people—would not that be a more honourable life for them than gaining precarious bread by 'bright effects'?"

One may reply, safely enough, that such a life is honourable in the sense that it is honest, but if the honour is that of which artists are most ambitious, it is equally safe to say that there is very little of it to be gained in that life. And this method of study has always been the basis of Ruskin's instruction — instruction for this and other reasons utterly wasted so far as the proper cultivation of art is concerned. I remember how, when Ruskin's drawing-book was published, an artist — whose feeling for all the nobler qualities of art I have rarely known equalled, and a personal friend and admirer of Ruskin, said to me, "He should not have printed that; we know now just what he does not know." It is not so much that he ignores the greater gifts, but that he conceives that they can be trained or developed by this kind of ant-like proceeding—going over the earth as an insect, not even as a bird. But it is in the comparison of the two painters whom he chooses as types that we most clearly recognise the failure to distinguish between the two forms of so-called art.

"Suppose, for instance, two men, equally honest, equally industrious, equally impressed with a humble desire to render some part of what they saw in nature faithfully, and otherwise trained in convictions such as I have above endeavoured to induce. But one of them is quiet in temperament, has a feeble memory, no invention, and excessively keen sight. The other is impatient in temperament, has a memory which nothing escapes, an invention which never rests, and is comparatively near-sighted. Set them both free in the same field in a mountain valley. One sees everything, small and large, with almost the same clearness; mountains and grasshoppers alike; the leaves on the branches, the veins on the pebbles, the bubbles in the stream; but he can remember nothing and invent nothing. Patiently he sets himself his mighty task; abandoning at once all thought of seizing transient effects, or giving general impressions of that which his eyes present to him in microscopical dissection, he chooses some small portion out of the infinite scene, and calculates with courage the number of weeks which must elapse before he can do justice to the intensity of his perceptions or the fullness of matter in his subject. Meanwhile, the other has been watching the change of the clouds and the march of the light along the mountain-sides; he beholds the whole scene in broad, soft masses of true gradation, *and the very feebleness of his sight is in some sort an advantage to him in making him more sensible of the aërial mystery of distance and hiding from him the multitudes of circumstances which it would have been impossible for him to represent.* . . . I have supposed the feebleness of sight in this last and of invention in the first painter, that the contrast between them may be the more striking; but with very slight modification both the characters are real. Grant to the first considerable inventive power with exquisite sense of colour, and give to the second, in addition to all his other faculties, the eye of an eagle, and the first is John Everett Millais, the second Joseph Mallord William Turner." "And thus Pre-Raphaelitism and Raphaelitism and Turnerism are all one and the same thing, so far as education can influence them; they are different in their choice, different in their faculties, but all the same in this, that Raphael himself, so far as he was great, and all who preceded or followed him who ever were great, became so by painting the truths around them as they appeared to each man's mind, not as he had been taught to see them except by the God who made both him and them."

And yet, between the first and last sentences which I have quoted, the author has gone through a detailed account of the development of Turner's art, showing that it was a continuous evolution of conventional forms of treatment borrowed from earlier painters. He is obliged, to complete his antithesis, to suppose Turner feeble of sight, because he could in no other way consistent with his theory (and everything is always bent to his theories) account for his ignoring "the multitudes of circumstances which it would have been impossible for him to represent," whereas the simple fact was that Turner had, as he afterwards admits, an eagle's eye, and simply ignored whatever in nature did not suit his purpose. Turner was bred on conventions; he began in the style of the men about him, Girtin and his kind; he went through the schools of Loutherbourg, Poussin, Claude, Vandervelde, imitating everybody except the most naturalistic of the Dutchmen, but never from the beginning to the end of his career painting from nature, or in any other way than from memory, and always in a conventional manner very much influenced by the early landscape painters of the true subjective school, to which he belonged in character, faculties, and method;

while Millais was a naturalist, who had no invention, no idealism, but was always working imitatively, and from direct vision, which Turner never did. Turner was influenced, and happily, by Claude to the last day of his life, though not always obeying the influence to the sa... apparent degree.

Of Ruskin the writer, aside from th... critic, it is surely superfluous for me to ... anything: for mastery of our language, the greater authorities long ago have given him his place; the multitude of petty critics and pinchbeck rhetoricians, who pay him the tribute of tawdry imitation, is the ever-present testimony to his power and masterhood. Probably no prose writer of this century has had so many choice extracts made from his writings—passages of gorgeous description, passionate exhortation, pathetic appeal, or apostolic denunciation; and certainly no one has so moulded the style of all the writers of a class as he, for there scarcely can be found a would-be art critic who does not struggle to fill his throat with Ruskin's thunders, so that a flood of Ruskin—and water—threatens all taste and all study of art. As an example of his diction take the description of "Schaffhausen":

"Stand for half an hour beside the Fall of Schaffhausen, on the north side where the rapids are long, and watch how the vault of water first bends, unbroken in *pure polished velocity*, over the arching rocks at the brow of the cataract, covering them with a dome of crystal twenty feet thick, so swift that its motion is unseen except when a foam globe from above darts over it like a falling star; and how the trees are lighted above it under all their leaves at the instant that it breaks into foam; and how all the hollows of that foam burn with green fire like so much shattering chrysoprase; and how ever and anon, startling you with its white flash, a jet of spray leaps hissing out of the fall like a rocket, bursting in the wind and driven away in dust, filling the air with light; and how, through the curdling wreaths of the restless crashing abyss below, the blue of the water, paled by the foam in its body, shows purer than the sky through white rain-cloud; while the *shuddering iris stoops in tremulous stillness over all, fading and flushing alternately through the choking spray and shattered sunshine,* hiding itself at last among the thick golden leaves, which toss to and fro in sympathy with the wild water; their dripping masses, lifted at intervals, like sheaves of loaded corn, by some stronger gush from the cataract, and bowed again upon the mossy rocks as its roar dies away; the dew gushing from their thick branches through drooping clusters of emerald herbage, and *sparkling in white threads along the dark rocks of the shore, feeding the lichens which chase and chequer them with purple and silver.*"

In the expression of what may be seen in a waterfall, and the suggestion of what may be felt, but seen by no bodily eye, is there anything in our language that is comparable to this? But is it fair to ask art to realise it? Who shall paint "the shuddering iris fading and flushing alternately through the choking spray and shattered sunshine?" It is beyond the province of art to emulate this vein of feeling, as much as to paint Shelley's "flames mingling with sunset." But how many hapless phaetons has our Apollo of the pen thus sent tumbling down on us, entangled in their "predicates and six," or sixty! Description à la Ruskin has become a disease of the literature of the generation, and your novelist coolly stops you in the crisis of his story to describe a sunset in two or three pages which, when all is said, compare with Ruskin as a satyr with Hyperion.

III

THUS Ruskin obstinately bent all his conclusions and observations to his doctrines—what he wanted to see he saw, nothing else. The summer before one of my early visits to England, I had painted a picture in what I believed the spirit of his teachings, being then one of the most enthusiastic of his disciples. I had conceived a death-struggle between a hunter and a buck, in which they had fallen together over a ledge of rock and lay in death at its foot. I had searched the forest around where I camped in the Adirondacks until I found the ledge which suited the conception, and painted it carefully, with the red sunset light coming aslant through the forest and falling on the perpendicular cliff, at the foot of which was a dense, dank growth of ferns, all painted on the spot and in the sunset light. At the foot, where they would fall, I put my guide, locked with a huge buck, and painted them as carefully as I knew how—the man from life and the buck immediately after I had killed him. I took it with me to London, and one day Ruskin came into my studio, and, seeing the picture, exclaimed with a gesture of disgust, "Why do you have this stinking carrion in your picture? Put it out, it's filthy, it stinks!" etc. I was too much under his influence to weigh his judgment against mine, and painted it out accordingly. Dante Rossetti, who had seen and liked the picture as it was, coming in again a few days after, exclaimed, "What have you done to your picture?" I explained, and with strong irritation in his manner he replied, "You've spoiled your picture," and walked straight out of the room. I *had* spoiled it; for everything in it had been chosen and painted with reference to this deadly duel, with which Ruskin had no sympathy. Death oppressed him, whence his annoyance with the picture; but that he was olfactorily impressed, as he was, could only be explained by the fact that, as always, he felt what he imagined or wished to see. He wanted to see truth in Turner's drawings, and he made his truth accordingly. I can but regard his influence on modern landscape painting as pernicious from beginning to end; and, coinciding as it did with the advent of a great naturalistic and, therefore, anti-artistic tendency in all branches of study, it was even more disastrous than it would have been in ordinary circumstances.

His architectural work, "Stones of Venice," etc., I am not so competent to judge, but I believe that, while on the one hand he did great good by bringing out the virtues of Gothic architecture and awakening the interest of the world in the art that was passing away, on the other hand he did harm by repressing the influence of the better form of Renaissance, which is often of the noblest and truest art, and is far more adapted to our modern ways of work and uses than is the Gothic. He uses here the same bitter polemics and biased judgment as in the "Modern Painters." In the lovely little Renaissance church of the Miracoli at Venice, where are the most exquisite decorations in that style of which I know, Ruskin finds among the arabesques *a child's head* tied by its locks among the tendrils of the vegetation, and inveighs bitterly against the brutality of such a conception as putting a bodiless head in the decoration. But he never stops to see that it is a cherub among other cherubim, and that, as it is in the character of the cherub to have no body, the tying of one of them by the hair to the vine is only a bit of playful invention in which there is no brutality whatever, but the most seraphic of practical jokes on the bodiless and helpless state of the charming little creature; a creature which, in Gothic days, might have been believed in as an actuality, but which the Renaissance only looked at as a fiction of mythology with the Tritons and Sirens, and therefore with no reverence. But with Greek art, all that in any way sympathised with its dominant character meets his anathema. It seems to me that even in architecture his influence is not catholic, but is tinged by his devotional tendencies, although he introduces an element of common sense into the criticism of architecture unknown before him.

But Ruskin's true position is higher than that of art critic in any possible development. It is as a moralist and a reformer, and in his passionate love of humanity (not inconsistent with much bitterness, and even unmerited, at times, to individual men) that we must recognise him. His place is in the pulpit, speaking largely and in the unsectarian sense. Truth is multiform, but of one essence, and, *such as he sees it*, he is always faithful to it. I have taken large exception to his ideas and teachings in respect to art because I feel that they are misleading. His mistakes in art are in some measure due to his fundamental mistake of measuring it by its moral powers and influence, and the roots of the error are so deeply involved in his character and mental development that it can never be uprooted. It is difficult for me (perhaps for any of his contemporaries) to judge him as a whole; because, besides being his contemporary and a sufferer by what I now perceive to be the fatal error of his system, I was for so many years his close personal friend; and because, while I do not agree with his tenets and am obliged by my own sense of right to combat many of his teachings, I still retain the personal affection for him of those years which are dear to memory, and reverence the man as I know him; and because I most desire that he should be judged rightly—as a man who, for moral greatness, has few equals in his day, and who deserves an honour and distinction which he has not received, and in a selfish and sordid world will not receive, but which I believe time will give him—that of being one who gave his whole life and substance to the furtherance of what he believed to be the true happiness and elevation of his fellow-men. Even were he the sound art critic so many people take him to be, his real nature rises above that office as much as humanity rises above art. When we wish to compare him with men of his kind, it must be with Plato or Savonarola rather than with Hazlitt or Hamerton. Art cannot be clearly estimated in any connection with morality, and Ruskin could never, any more than Plato or Savonarola, escape the condition of being in every fibre of his nature a moralist and not an artist, and as he advanced in life the ethical side of his nature more and more asserted its mastery, though less and less in theological terms.

If I have assumed the right to pass judgment on his art teachings, it is because I have devoted most of my life to the study of art and more years than Ruskin had when he finished his most important books; but when I come to the moral problem, so vast, so profound and momentous in comparison with any questions of culture, I have not the presumption to judge a man whose moral nature I know to be so exceptional, and winged to flights that I can only honour from below. Here we enter into a world where only the Judge of all life can pronounce and where my opinion must be respectful, for the unquestionable loftiness and unselfishness of his nature, and the consecration of his life to the advancement of truth as he has seen it, give him, to me, an authority I dare not debate with, and which I insist on all the more because I know the world does not accord it to him. No one has yet dared answer Pilate, and I have no disposition to judge whether Ruskin's social reforms and political theories are in accordance with eternal truth or not—whether they are practical or not is, perhaps, a question of epoch simply.

As an indication of Ruskin's position—more free, possibly, because more personal than those given in his early works—I quote part of one of his first letters to me (about 1851). I had been involved in mystical speculation, partly growing out of the second volume of "Modern Painters," and had written to him for counsel.

"I did not, indeed, understand the length to which your views were carried when I saw you here, or I should have asked you much more about them than I did; and your present letter leaves me still thus far in the dark that I do not know whether you only have a strong conviction that there is such a message to be received from all things, or whether in any sort you think you have understood and can interpret it, for how otherwise should your persuasion of the fact be so strong? I never thought of such a thing being possible before, and now that you have suggested it to me I can only imagine that by rightly understanding as much of the nature of everything as ordinary watchfulness will enable any man to perceive, we might, if we looked for it, find in everything some special moral lesson or type of particular truth, and that then one might find a language in the whole world before unfelt like that which is forever given to the ravens or to the lilies of the field by Christ's speaking of them. This, I think, you might very easily accomplish so far as to give the first idea and example; then it seems to me that every thoughtful man who succeeded you would be able to add some types or words to the new language, but all this quite independently of any Mystery in the Thing or Inspiration in the Person, any more than there is Mystery in the cleaning of a Room covered with dust—of which you remember Bunyan makes so beautiful a spiritual application, so that one can never more see the thing done without being interested. If there be mystery in things requiring revelation, I cannot tell on what terms it might be vouchsafed us, nor in any way help you to greater certainty of conviction, but my advice to you would be on no account to agitate nor grieve yourself nor look for inspiration—for assuredly many of our noblest English minds have been entirely overthrown by doing so—but to go on doing what you are quite sure is right; that is, striving for constant purity of thought, purpose and word: not on any account overworking yourself—especially in headwork—but accustoming yourself to look for the spiritual meaning of things just as easily to be seen as their natural meaning; and fortifying yourself against the hardening effect of your society, by good literature. You should read much—and generally old books; but above all avoid *German* books—and all Germanists except Carlyle, whom read as much as you can or like: read George Herbert and Spenser and Wordsworth and Homer, all constantly; Young's "Night Thoughts," Crabbe—and, of course, Shakespeare, Bacon and Jeremy Taylor and Bunyan; do not smile if I mention also

"Robinson Crusoe" and the "Arabian Nights," for standard places on your shelves. I say read Homer: I do not know if you can read Greek, but I think it would be healthy work for you to teach it to yourself if you cannot, and then I would add to my list Plato—but I cannot conceive a good translation of Plato. I had nearly forgotten one of the chief of all—Dante. But in doing this, do not strive to keep yourself in an elevated state of spirituality. No man who earnestly believed in God and the next world was ever petrified or materialised in heart, whatever society he kept. Do whatever you can, however simple or commonplace, in your art; do not force your spirituality on your American friends. Try to do what they admire as well as they would have it, unless it cost you too much—but do not despise it because commonplace. Do not strive to do what you feel to be above your strength. God requires that of no man. Do what you feel happy in doing: mingle some physical science with your imaginative studies; and be sure that God will take care to lead you into the fulfilment of whatever tasks he has ready for you, and will show you what they are in his own time.

"Thank you for your sketch of American art. I do hope that your countrymen will look upon it, in time, as all other great nations have looked upon it at their greatest times, as an object for their united aim and strongest efforts. I apprehend that their deficiency in landscape has a deep root—the want of historical associations. Every year of your national existence will give more power to your landscape painting—then, do you not want architecture? Our children's taste is fed with Ruins of Abbeys. I believe the first thing you have to do is to build a few Arabic palaces by way of novelty—one brick of jacinth and one of jasper. . . .

"Write to me whenever you are at leisure and think I can be of use to you—with sympathy or in any way, and believe me always interested in your welfare and very faithfully yours, J. RUSKIN."

I could not quote from his published works so condensed a summary of the creed of the man: it maintains the supremacy of the moral element which has obtained in his life-work taken as a whole.

That comparatively few people have read the "Fors Clavigera" I know, for, having occasion to complete my set not long since, I found that several of the numbers supplied me by the publisher were from the first thousand, published years ago; and yet, this is the work which more than any other gives us a clear insight into the character and mental tendencies of Ruskin. He is here at his ease, not bound by any prepossessions and theories; wayward, outspoken, indifferent to praise or blame; speaking with full possession of himself and frank appreciation of his audience, addressing himself "to the workmen and labourers of Great Britain," not so much in the hope that they would come to fill his school, but because he knew that only by the poor and the despised by the great world was there any hope of the reconstruction of society, as he dreamed it, being effected or accepted. The drift of all Ruskin's preaching (and I use the word in its noble sense) is a protest against materialism in ourselves, impurity in our studies and desires, and selfishness in our conduct towards our fellowmen.

He considers himself the pupil of Carlyle—for me, he floats in a purer air than Carlyle ever breathed. As a feminine nature he was captivated by the robust masculine force of his great countryman, and there was, in the imperial theory of Carlyle, much that chimed with Ruskin's own ideas of human government. The Chelsean, regretfully looking back to the day of absolutism and brutal domination of the appointed king, was, in a certain sense, a sympathetic reply to Ruskin's longings for a firm and orderly government when he felt the quicksands of the transitional order of the day yielding under his feet; but, in reality, the two regarded Rule from points as far removed from each other as those of Luther and Voltaire. Carlyle's ideal was one of a Royal Necessity, an incarnate law indifferent to the crushed in its marchings and rulings — burly, brutal, contemptuous of the luckless individual or the overtaken straggler; his Rule exists not for the sake of humanity, but for that of Order, as if Order and Rule were called out for their own sake; he puffs into perdition the trivial details of individual men, closing accounts by ignoring the fractions. Ruskin loses sight of no detail, but calls in to the benefit of *his* Order and Rule every child and likeness of a child in larger form, full of a tenderness which is utterly human yet inexhaustible. Carlyle's Ruler is like a Viking's god, his conception utterly pagan; Ruskin's is Christlike; Carlyle's word is like the mace of Charlemagne, Ruskin's like the sword of the Angel Gabriel; if Ruskin is notably egotistical, Carlyle is utterly selfish; if Ruskin dogmatises like an Evangelist, Carlyle poses as a Prophet; and the difference, when we come to sum up all the qualities, moral, intellectual, and literary, seems to me to be in favour of Ruskin. Their ideals are similarly antithetical — Ruskin's lying in a hopeful future, an unattainable Utopia, perhaps, but still a blessed dream; Carlyle's in a return to a brutal and barren past, made forever impossible by the successful assertion of human individuality, and for whose irrevocability we thank God with all our hearts and in all hope of human progress. The public estimate has not overrated Ruskin, just as he had not overrated Turner, because the aggregate impression of power received was adequate to the cause; but in the one case, as in the other, the mistake has been relative, and consisted in mis-estimating the genius and attributing the highest value to the wrong item in the aggregate. I may be mistaken in my estimate of Ruskin, but I believe that the future will exalt him above it rather than depress him below it.

A FEW OF LOWELL'S LETTERS

It has been repeatedly said in my hearing, by men who had come to know Lowell personally, after having known his works, that he was better than anything he had done. No one knew this so well as those who knew him best. I made my acquaintance with his works in the days of early artistic enthusiasms, when I used to visit the studio of William Page, the poet's intimate friend and ardent admirer, to whose almost inspired (oracular, certainly) improvisations on art and poetry I used to listen till my young blood ran quick, and my own enthusiasms made me see what was never to be seen again, even in dreams. Page used to recite Lowell's poems with his own commentary, so subtly fantastic at times that it made one think he had taken part in the composition of the poet's text, or thought he had, at least. I only remember as then in print the volume of early poems, and the Sir Launfal in a small separate volume. There was much in the poems which appealed powerfully to the green and sentimental stage of mental growth in which I then was, and I learned most of them by heart, together with the Sir Launfal. I spent the following autumn at a lighthouse on the coast of New England, studying the sea in its multiform phases, and the two volumes were all the literature I carried with me. But I remember saying, about that time, to a common friend of Page and myself, that the author wanted only the ripening of a great sorrow to bring out his greater powers. The poems seemed to me, even then, only the overflow of a mind so full of poetic thought that verse flowed from it as water from a deep spring, giving out what would run to waste if not turned to some direct use.

It was not long after this that my criticism was to be tested by life. Lowell's wife died, leaving him in that gloom from which came the series of short poems, to my mind the best expression of the finest side of the man's nature—"The Wind-Harp," "Auf Wiedersehen," "Palinode," "Ode to Happiness," and "The Dead House,"*— expressions of the passion of bereavement at work in a strong and healthy nature, not crushed, but bowed down; for he was under the influence of a sane and elastic sorrow which did not paralyse, but turned his mental activity to the presentation of the overpowering passion, genuine, pure, and without a trace of the artifice or inflation of the aftermath of grief. The only thing that I know in English poetry which affects me similarly, is the "Break, break, break" of

* There are, amongst the poems written previous to this date, two which are of the same passion, and due to the death of his little daughter Rose. But even in those there is a measure of restraint, as if the bereavement were tempered by participation. They do not go to the very depths of the man's nature as do the "Wind-Harp" and "Ode to Happiness."

Tennyson, and there the freshness of passion has given place to the consciousness of art and the study of form. It was in this phase of his life that I made Lowell's acquaintance.

I was about commencing the publication—in company with John Durand, son of a former president of the Academy of Design—of an art journal, *The Crayon*, and went to Cambridge to solicit the assistance of those writers whose work in any way sympathised with the object of our journal. If I remember rightly, I had no letter of introduction, but presented myself on the strength of my mission, and was received by Lowell with the princely courtesy which was his manner. I was full of my project, which seemed to me, in my enthusiasm, evangelical; for I was set to preach and labour for the revival of art, and he accepted me on my own ground, with entire sympathy. One of his letters, written a little later, when our acquaintance had ripened into friendship, has such a significance as a revelation of the state of his mind at that time, that I do not believe I need apologise for introducing it, though it is very personal to me; it would not tell its story if I left out the personal part. I wanted something of his for the opening number of the paper, and he had sent me a passage from his "Pictures from Appledore," which he entitled "August Afternoon." I wanted him to be on board at "the launch," and I had also a poem of Bryant's, that called "A Rain Dream" in his published volume; but the scheme of the journal did not admit more than one such notable contribution in each number, so I had to choose between Bryant and Lowell as the poet of the occasion. It is to this that he alludes in the letter.

GRUB STREET, 7*th Dec'r*, 1854.

MY DEAR SIR,—I am sorry to have kept your proofs so long, but I was absent from home the day they came.

I don't know now whether I sent you the right part of the poem, but I wished to give you the most *paletty* part first; and I am now so overwhelmed with lectures and Grub Street that I have literally not time to copy the introductory verses describing the island. But, my dear sir, if Bryant has given you a poem, you should put that in your first number, by all means. It will do you more good than many of mine, and your first duty is to your *Crayon*-child, wherever you are not obliged to sacrifice any principle to it. Don't mind me in the least. *I* wish your journal to succeed. Remember that success is the only atmosphere through which your ideas will look lovely to the public you wish to influence. Bryant's name will help you more than mine; therefore, take him first. Not that I like to give up my place on board at the launch, either, for I am sure it will be a graceful one.

You mustn't talk of Christmas gifts and things. I shall think you mean to keep me in Grub Street in spite of myself. [I had intended to send his daughter something for Christmas, and suppose

I must have asked some question about her tastes.]
I positively will not be paid in any way, if I may say so after being more than paid by your beautiful drawings, which M. likes as well as I do, and declares a preference for the larger one, "On the" —— I can't make out the name, but I shall call it the Lethe, that drowsy water with tree-dreams in it, so smooth and sleek and soaked with sun, it seems a drink of it would quench the thirst of all sad memories. Only, no Lethe *can*, for we are our own saddest memories — a hundred a day. I thank you for them most heartily, and for your letter as well.

I am glad you had a pleasant time here. *I* had, and you made me fifteen years younger while you stayed. When a man gets to my age, enthusiasms don't often knock at the door of his garret. I am all the more charmed with them when they come. A youth full of such pure intensity of hope and faith and purpose, what is he but the breath of a resurrection-trumpet to us stiffened old fellows, bidding us up out of our clay and earth if we would not be too late?

Your inspiration is still to you a living mistress; make her immortal in her promptings and her consolations by imaging her truly in art. Mine looks at me with eyes of paler flame and beckons across a gulf. You came into my loneliness like an incarnate aspiration. And it is dreary enough sometimes; for a mountain peak, on whose snow your foot makes the first mortal print, is not so lonely as a room full of happy faces from which *one* is missing forever. This was originally the fifth stanza of "The Wind-Harp":

> "O tress that so oft on my heart hath lain,
> Rocked to rest within rest by its thankful beating,
> Say, which is harder,—to bear the pain
> Of laughter and light, or to wait in vain,
> 'Neath the unleaved tree, the impossible meeting?
> If Death's lips be icy, Life gives, I wis,
> Some kisses more clay-cold and darkening than his!"

Forgive me, but you spoke of it first. [I had in a letter spoken of "The Wind-Harp," which he had read to me, on my visit already alluded to, in its then incomplete state.]

I have done better than send you a poem; I have got you—a subscriber. On this momentous topic I shall enlarge no further than to say that I wish to be put on your list also in my capacity as gentleman, and not author. I will not be deadheaded. I respect my profession too much. . . .

Heartily and hopefully yours,

J. R. LOWELL.

It is forty-five years since that letter was written, but I can never read it again without the reflection, pale though it be, of the pathos which rests on that visit to his study when he read me "The Wind-Harp," and we sat silent long into the twilight of the autumn day, the bare boughs of the elm-trees outside his windows cutting against the sky; and his little daughter came in after her lessons. When she left the room, I spoke of the delicate chiselling of her features, and he replied by pointing to her mother's portrait on the study wall.

Perhaps I overrate my own way of looking at Lowell, but in that letter there seems the expression of his character, writ large. Out of the depth of the shadow over his life, in the solitude of his study, with nothing but associations of his wrecked happiness permitted around him, the kindly sympathy with a new aspiration wakened him to a momentary gaiety, his humour flashed out irrepressible, and his large heart turned its warmest side to the new friend, who came only to make new calls on his benevolence; that is, to give him another opportunity to bestow himself on others. There is in it the generosity, the pathos, the subtle humour, the worldly wisdom, and the self-forgetfulness which we who knew him recognise, drawn against the dark background of his bereaved life. There was in Lowell no distinction to be found between the man and the poet. What he wrote he felt. No line of his but was the glow of what he felt and acted to his fellow-men. It is possible, therefore, that for us who knew him, and to whom his sunny nature showed its warmest side, it is impossible to see his work as it will be seen by those who did not know him. It would be quite impossible for me to criticise Lowell's work as I could that of a man I never knew; the halo of his personality surrounds the object of criticism and makes the critical vision indistinct. I loved the man with a passion no other man had ever awakened in me, one which often recalled to me the love of David for Jonathan.

The letter, at this long distance, confounds itself with the visit which preceded it. I had stayed with him at Elmwood, and we had talked of many things which provoke confidence, had visited his favourite bits of landscape in the classic fields, Beaver Brook, the Waverley Oaks, etc., and, in the dusk of the day, chance, or some spiritual induction, had led him into speaking of his griefs, charily, half apologetically; and when a man can speak of his griefs to another, there are two ties established, one of a sympathy in them, and the other of that lightening of the soul from the putting them into words, which seems to incur an obligation where really one is conferred. It was in this confidence that he read me the "Ode to Happiness," the first full expression of his sorrow he had made to me; and I quite broke down, and stole to the window to hide my tears. Perhaps certain trivial troubles of my own, but which, at the time, seemed to me as grave as death, put me in tune with his mood, and so our friendship found its first minor chord.

Nothing would have induced me to take his advice and give any other the place I intended for him at "the launch," so the first number of *The Crayon* contained the bit of his "Appledore" study, of which he sent me two more fragments later on. He took the liveliest interest in the paper as long as I remained at the head of it, and, amongst other things, wrote for it the

"Invita Minerva," in the proof-correcting of which he allowed himself one of the quaint, and to my mind delightful, bits of eccentric diction he was so fond of, but rarely indulged in. The second line, which in the collected poems stands,

"The pennon'd reeds, that, as the west wind blew,"

was so written originally; but, in the correction of proof, was changed to "in the west wind blue," and was so printed in *The Crayon*.

The next letter I have from him—for the minor letters and the manuscripts seem all to have gone to the autograph-hunters—is dated the week after *The Crayon* had been launched. I have no recollection of what I had written, but I do remember that on reading the "Auf Wiedersehen," printed in one of the magazines of the day— I think Putnam's,—I sent him some verses which that poem called out, and in which, possibly, I had tried, not to console, for the folly of that I even then knew, but to mingle a sympathetic pain with his.

ELMWOOD, 11*th Jan.* 1855.

MY DEAR FRIEND,—I fear you have thought me very cold and ungrateful not to have answered sooner (if it were only with God bless you) your very kind and tender letter. I cannot say more of it than that it came to my heart like the words of a woman. I need not write how entirely grateful I am for it.

I have delayed writing till I found a chance to copy some more "Appledore" for you. I have sent a tolerably long bit this time, for I suppose you will like something to fill up as much as may be. So, look upon it as a large canvas that will at least cover bare wall. I have had your two drawings framed, and they hang up now on the inside of my door, and please everybody that sees them, me above all.

I have been fearfully busy with my lectures! And so nervous about them, too! I had never spoken in public. There was a great rush for tickets (the lectures were *gratis*), only one in five of the applicants being supplied, and altogether I was quite taken aback. I had no idea that there would be such a desire to hear me.

I delivered my first lecture to a crowded hall on Tuesday night, and I believe I have succeeded. The lecture was somewhat abstract, but I kept the audience perfectly still for an hour and a quarter. (They are in the habit of going out at the end of the hour.) I delivered it again yesterday to another crowd, and was equally successful; so I think I am safe now. But I have six yet to write, and am consequently very busy and pressed for time.

I felt anxious, of course, for I had a double responsibility. The lectures [before the Lowell Institute] were founded by a cousin of mine, and the trustee is another cousin; so I wished not only to do credit to myself and my name, but to justify my relative in appointing me to lecture.

It is all over now, and as far as the public is

concerned I have succeeded; but the lectures keep me awake and make me lean.

I am quite sensible now that I did not do Mr. Bryant justice in the Fable. But there was [no personal feeling in what I said, though I have regretted what I did say because it might seem personal. I am now asked to write a review of his poems for the *North American*. If I do, I shall try to do him justice.

I think he has been more fortunate in Flemish pictures than I, if he does not find in "Appledore" a sentiment that is wanting in them. One of the best fragments is yet to come. . . .

Yours,   J. R. LOWELL.

His allusion to Bryant was due to my having told him that the latter was always a little sore at Lowell's treatment of him in the Fable for Critics, and especially at the lines which became a commonplace of criticism:—

> "If he stir you at all, it is just, on my soul,
> Like being stirred up with the very North Pole;"

and as, just before taking charge of *The Crayon*, I had been on the staff of Bryant's *Evening Post* and on friendly terms with the poet, I had become aware of the impression, and desired to efface it. The opportunity occurred a little later, on the occasion of Lowell's departure for Europe, when I gave him a dinner in New York, to which I invited Bryant; and seating them together, with no regard to precedence (they had never seen each other before), I left them to themselves. Though there were of the company Charles Sumner, C. F. Briggs (Harry Franco), Whipple, Bayard Taylor, and other of Lowell's old friends, he devoted himself to Bryant the entire evening, and completely fascinated him. Anxious to gather the elder poet's impression, I left Lowell and Taylor at Oscanyan's Café smoking their nargilehs, and walked home with Bryant, soon satisfying myself. The criticism of Bryant on the "Appledore," in which he spoke of it as like a Flemish picture in its fidelity, was not intended to be one of disparagement, though Lowell so regarded it.

Those who have no acquaintance with the literary life of the day I am dealing with, can hardly understand how limited then was the range of Lowell's possession of the public. It was usual, amongst his friends, to speak of him as the "most Shakespearean man since Shakespeare"; but, by the American public even, he was hardly held as more than a brilliant dilettante. His carelessness of the form of his earlier work, his evident slight estimation of it, and the extraordinary ease with which it was thrown off, all contributed to this impression. The Biglow Papers were political squibs, of the true position of which, as literature, no one then had a just conception, blown about as the papers were in the winds which grew to the great tempest of our civil war, and they were read with partisan eyes. The Fable for Critics was limited in its range of audience, and, treated as a controversial and personal *jeu d'esprit*, attacked and defended without serious study; while the serious poems were so unequal, and, as he afterwards recognised, in some cases so unworthy his powers, that they diminished the impression of the mass of his work. He set so little value on what cost him no labour —for he wrote verse more easily than prose— that he never gave himself the trouble of polishing or pruning, and the early volume contains much that is juvenile and open to sharp criticism, rendered all the more certain by his own pungency as critic. He knew his own value, as we know it now, but it was the value in *posse* which he felt; for his work of the moment he had little concern. Had he held more conceit of his verse and more anxiety about public opinion, he certainly would have suppressed much of his early work, to his better reputation in later years. The lectures referred to in the letter last quoted showed him in another light, and justified the faith of his friends in his large intellectual possessions. They drove him into deep water, and he was obliged to swim *in mare magno*; their preparation involved work which, in his melancholy and loneliness, was necessary to bring him out of the morbid condition into which he had fallen when I first knew him. He had become hypochondriacal, and, at the time of my first visit, had begun to nurse imaginary ills, and brooded much by himself, with a hopeless feeling as to his future condition, which he made no effort to throw off. The lectures forcibly brought him up out of the depths, and he resumed his normal life. With all his strength of feeling and impulsive activity, his was too healthy a nature to remain long in morbid conditions, and once he had set about resisting them he rapidly returned to healthy work. On the 25th of January, a fortnight later than the last letter, he wrote me:

". . . I came very near forgetting my proof sheets altogether, but I have delivered five of my lectures now, and on Friday shall have half finished my course. Meanwhile, I have only a week's start, so that I have to work hard; what with inevitable interruptions. . . .

"Do not think that I feel the less interest in you and yours because I write such scrawls. I am not used to being tied to hours or driven. I have always waited on the good genius, and he will not come for being sent after by express; so I am in a *feeze* half the time."

And a few days later, but without date except "Elmwood," he says:—

"I shall have done grinding for the Philistines next Saturday, and it will give me, I need not say, the greatest pleasure to see you. . . . I have been meaning for some time to write you a word, merely to say that Longfellow told me the other day that he would send you the first poem he had that was suitable for your purpose. Perhaps he has written; if not, I shall be glad to be the herald.

"You will like to hear (but it is at present a semi-secret) that I am to be nominated next

Thursday to fill Longfellow's place in the college. It was all very pleasant, for the place sought me, and not I it.

"I have only to deliver two courses of lectures in the year; have all the rest of the time to myself, and the salary will make me independent. If the overseers of the college confirm the appointment of the Corporation (of which there is little doubt), I shall go abroad for a year to Germany and Spain to acquire the languages.

"So, by the time you come, I shall probably be Professor Lowell, at your service, and shall expect immense respect in consequence. Take care after that how you squire or mister me. I have not discovered the dulness of *The Crayon*, and only hope its point will be sharp enough to draw the public. If I go to Berlin, I will send you some sketches of the gallery there. Spain, too, is rich."

He was so scornful of money, when his friends were concerned, that he seemed to be independent of his labour; but we see the satisfaction with which he welcomes the independence of the salaried professor, and I am sure that the greater feeling in his own mind was that he could afford to be more generous. I never heard him speak of money except to refuse to be paid it, and in the above communication. At that moment of my life, I was perhaps better prepared to be liberal with him than he with me, but any compensation beyond a drawing or study from nature was always absolutely refused to the last of our journalistic relations; and when, later in life, fortune left me on the shoals, he insisted on putting me, on occasion, on my feet again, with all the love of a brother and the delicacy of a poet, and always with some excuse of an unexpected good fortune which he wished to partake with some one.

"Greater than anything he ever did," they used to say; but how much greater, and how much nobler than any work can be, no one knows so well as I. His heart ran even with his brain, and, when there was a chance, outran it. He had twin faults: he under-estimated his own work, and tinted that of his friends with the colours of his esteem. In one of the exhibitions of our National Academy, I had a large study of a bit of Adirondack forest and lake, of which one of the critics had spoken in strongly damnatory terms, and Lowell wrote me of it:—

ELMWOOD, 21*st May* 1855.

MY DEAR FRIEND,—" It being granted that the earth is a hollow cube"—"But I beg your pardon, my dear sir, I granted no such thing." "Well, then, it being necessary to the purposes of this argument that the earth *should be* a hollow cube, which is precisely the same thing, I go on to demonstrate," etc.

Now, what does he mean by saying that your picture is "an *unpleasingly* grouped assemblage of *unpleasing* natural objects?" Is a hemlock trunk unpleasing? Is the silvery-grey bole of a sloping birch unpleasing? Is the beech stem, plashed with wavering pools of watery sunshine, unpleasing? And pray tell me how, in a picture, a thing *can* be "literally rendered." There is no such matter possible. The closer the imitation, in giving rounded or irregular shapes, perspective, etc., on a flat surface, the greater have been the difficulties overcome, and the greater the imagination in being able to see things as they truly are, and not as they seem. To make a model of a beech stem is quite another affair. We would rather have a section of the real thing. Is there not a difference even in daguerreotypes in favour of the man who is enough of an artist to choose the right moment and point of view? And even were the tree trunk a deformed one, were it ever so ugly, mis-shapen, warty, scrofulous, carious, what you will, it is one of the curious psychological facts that it is yet not unpleasing. For, while any *lusus naturæ* in anything that breathes is hateful, a fanciful resemblance to the diseases and deformities of animal life in anything that merely grows appeals at once to our sense of the odd, the humorous, the grotesque; or else is not disagreeable, because it is a likeness upward and not downward. But this glances toward a deeper deep, and I forbear. Anyhow, I like your picture and the idea of it; only, you must make interest with Aquarius to water your lake a little. But

> "When they talked of their Raphaels, Correggios, and stuff,
> He shifted his trumpet, and only took snuff."

Or, let me translate a proverb from the Feejee dialect:—

> "That which we like, likes us:
> No need of any fuss."

Nay, take this other, which I this moment copy from the walls of a house just unburied at Pompeii :—

> "Perchance the thing I banish, me expels;
> Be chary, ostracizer, of your shells!
> Madman, thou deem'st thyself sublimely free,
> And ly'st on straw in that crampt cell of Thee."

Or, perhaps, this is a better translation of the last couplet :—

> "Thou deem'st thyself a King, poor crazy elf,
> Chained to the wall of that crampt cell, Thyself."

The Feejee Islanders (who love curried Calvinists and minced missionary) and the Pompeians (who got up such suicidal fireworks for the entertainment of Admiral Pliny) knew a thing or two, nevertheless!

It is a glorious, blue, north-westerly sky; the oak woods are pink with buds; the linnets, catbirds, fire-hangbirds, and robins are all singing hymeneals to the Spring, and she trembles through all her wreaths of new-born leaves and seems equally pleased with each of them. She does not say, "Oh, Linnet, put yourself to school with Maestro Catbird," nor "Be silent, Robin, my boy, till you can sing like Signor Robert of Lincoln." *Per Bacco!* did not brave Masaccio paint St Peter right in the streets of Florence, working a miracle with vulgar Florentines all about him, and did not Raphael and Michael say that the Brancacci chapel was their school? . . .

In a letter of a little earlier date (10th of May 1855) he gives another instance of his constant thoughtfulness for others:—

". . . I saw Longfellow yesterday, and reminded him of his promise to send you a poem; and he renewed it, but said that he had not anything he liked well enow to send. I told him that it did not much matter for a long poem, and that his name would be of service to *The Crayon* now that it was seeking an introduction to the world. I know that he means rightly, and only hope that he will send you something while it can be of commercial advantage to you. Don't be shocked at my market-place view of the thing; I feel as wise as a woman when I find anybody with a beard who seems a worse manager than I, and one has a right to be shrewd for his friend. Meanwhile, I send you some verses of my own, which you may like or not, as you please. They are very much at your service if you want them, and perhaps Professor Lowell's name may be of use. . . . As soon as we have a leaf or two I shall expect a visit from you. I will write and let you know when our winter is over. Our spring is like that delicacy, a frozen plum pudding, which cheats every uninitiated person into an impromptu toothache. It looks as if it ought to be hot, and it is Nova Zembla focussed."

Following these letters there is a wide gap in my file. I have no memorandum of the time of his sailing for Germany, but in the letter of May 10th he says, "Think of anything I can do for you on the other side. I go to Germany first"; and the next letter I have is dated from Dresden. I was overworked on *The Crayon*, and he on his German studies; for he was not a man to do less than his utmost when he had accepted his duty. But this is dated October 14, 1855, and shows already the renewed intellectual activity at full swing. The wit and humour, which in our first acquaintance only flashed out in intervals of gloom, begin to take the upper hand again.

. . . You may lay it to anything you like, except my having forgotten you, that I have not written sooner. I have thought of you only too much, for I wished, when I wrote, to send you something for *The Crayon*; and not finding aught to write about, you began to haunt me and shake your printer's-inky locks at me—only, unhappily, the case was the reverse of Banquo's, since thou couldst say I'd not done it. Now, this would not do. I would not have a friendship which I value so much, more than any contracted in these later years, associated with any uneasy thought. So I resolved to lay the ghost at once, as we can all *blue* ghosts that haunt us, in a sea of ink. What have I to say that I had not a month ago? Nothing; but then I will write and manfully say so. I can, at least, tell you how warm a feeling I have towards you, and that is something. But for *The Crayon*? That we will see presently. First, I must thank you for the likeness of yourself, which you may be sure I am glad to have with me, and for your letters. Only, why so short? One would think you were writing across Broadway instead of the Atlantic. But I will give it a good turn by thinking that you do not feel me far away from you, as truly I am not. About Griswold and the rest of it I understand nothing, and care as little, unless for its troubling you. When I get over here, it is the Styx that is between me and America. I have drunk Lethe water to wash down Nepenthe with, and have forgotten everything but my friends, like a happy shade. What care we careless spirits for what troubled us in the flesh? "My little man," says Wordsworth to Pope, when they meet in the Fortunate Islands, "I am sorry to say"— the wretch! he is not sorry a bit— "that your poems are not so much read as once." "My what? Ah! poems—yes, I think I *did* write some things once. And so they don't read 'em, eh? 'Tis all one for that—I wouldn't read 'em myself. Come in, Mr—a—a—I beg your pardon—ah, Woodwarth? Yes, come in, Mr Woodwarth, and try the Lethe: 'tis the best spring in the place; and you will meet some eminent characters in the pump-room." So it goes. Give yourself no more trouble about the picture. As it is one, I suppose I may say *hang* the picture! But I dare be sworn you have forgotten all about it by this time.

But for *The Crayon*—what have I seen? Why, I have seen the Van Eyck at Ghent, and liked it so well that I have never a word to say about it. And I saw the Memlings at Bruges—what a place it is! a bit of Italy drifted away northward and stranded like an erratic boulder in Flanders—and I liked those so well that I am equally dumb thereanent. And I saw the Rubenses in Antwerp, which have all been skinned alive by the restorers, and which they have put into a little room fenced off from the cathedral, so that they may get a *franc* out of every stranger who comes there— the Jews! "Is not my Father's house a house of prayer? But ye have made it a den of thieves." There has been great power and passion in those pictures—Rubens is a poem translated out of Low Dutch into Italian; but in the little doghole where they are, one cannot see them. What was meant to be seen at forty feet shall one see at fifteen? Offer a man a magnifying-glass to look at an elephant with! Somehow I feel inclined to say "He was a great *gentleman*, that Rubens," but great *man* seems a little too much. But great he surely was in some sense or other—you feel that. Then I saw all the Dutch pictures at the Hague; but I think that Rembrandt, the greatest imagination these low countries ever produced, is better seen here in Dresden, than at the Hague. As for Paul Potter's famous *Bull*, it is no more to be compared with Rosa Bonheur's *Horse Fair* than a stuffed and varnished dolphin with a living one. Here there are some wonderful pictures. Titian's *Tribute-Money* is marvellously great; the head of Christ the noblest and most pathetic I have ever seen, full of a magnificent sadness. There is also a truly delicious Claude, and deep rock-embedded bay so liquidly dark and cool! There is a

Holy Family by Holbein, too, pathetically prosaic. I forgot to speak of an Albert Dürer at the Hague, a portrait of the future emperor (Maximilian, I think) as a child of three years, with an apple in his hand instead of the globe of empire which was afterward, if I remember, so heavy for him. Is it not a pretty fancy? But I have really got something for *The Crayon*—this is not, but must wait till next week's mail—an account of a visit I made to Retsch. It is late now, and I am not in a good mood, either. I have heard bad news—not of M., thank God!

You might make an item out of this—that the King of Saxony allows no copies to be made in the gallery, in order that the artists here may choose original subjects and paint them out of their own experience. Also Bendemann (their best painter here) is making a good picture, very pure and classic, out of the meeting of Ulysses with Nausicaa, in the Odyssey. But I must say good-night and God bless you! I have so much writing of German to do that my eyes can't bear much night work, and it is near twelve. Sunday is my only holiday. Next week, then. . . .

The visit to Retsch never came. Lowell always planned more than any mortal man could do; he laid schemes of work like bridges with one abutment in time and the other in eternity. He had too much to do, and I, on the other side, became so overborne by my editorial duties—*The Crayon* going to leeward all the time then — that our correspondence flagged. The next word I have from him shows the man overworked and dejected, but doing his duty to his position.

DRESDEN, 18th Feb'y 1856.

MY DEAR FRIEND,—I reproach myself bitterly for not having sooner answered your letter, but what is the use of spurring an already beaten-out horse? What energy can self-reproach communicate to a man who has barely resolution enough to do what is necessary for the day, and who shoves everything else over into the never-coming to-morrow? To say all in one word, I have been passing a very wretched winter. I have been out of health and out of spirits, gnawed a great part of the time by an insatiable home-sickness, and deprived of my usual means of ridding myself of bad thoughts by putting them into verse; for I have always felt that I was here for the specific end of learning German, and not of pleasing myself.

Just now I am better in body and mind. My cure has been wrought by my resolving to run away for a month into Italy. Think of it— Italy! I shall see Page and Norton and the grave of our little Walter.* I can hardly believe that I am going, and in ten days.

What you tell me about *The Crayon,* you may be sure fills me with a very sincere regret. It does not need to tell you how much interest

---

* Lowell's little boy, who died at Rome, and is buried in the Protestant cemetery there.

I took in it and you; and, what is better, my interest in it was not that merely of a friend of yours, but sprang from a conviction that it would do much for the æsthetic culture of our people. I am very sorry on every account that it is to be given up. I had hoped so much from it. It is a consolation to me that you will be restored to the practice instead of the criticism and exposition of art, and that we shall get some more pictures like the one which took so strong a hold of me in the New York exhibition. I shall hope to become the possessor of one myself, after I get quietly settled again at Elmwood with the Old Man of the Sea of my first course of lectures off my shoulders. You must come and make me a visit, and I will show you some nice studies of landscape in our neighbourhood, and especially one bit of primitive forest that I know within a mile and a half of our house.

I have been studying like a dog—no, dogs don't study, I mean a learned pig—this winter, and I think my horizon has grown wider, and that when I come back I shall be worth more to my friends. I have learned the boundaries of my knowledge, and *Terra Incognita* does not take so much space on my maps. In German, I have every reason to be satisfied with my progress, though I should have learned more of the colloquial language if I had had spirits enough to go into any society. But already the foreboding of Italy fills me with a new life and soul. I feel as if I had been living with no outlook on my south side, and as if a wall had been toppled over which had darkened all my windows in that direction. Bodily and spiritually I have suffered here with cold, but, God be thanked, it will soon be over.

My great solace (or distraction) has been the theatre, which is here excellent. I not only get a lesson in German, but I have learned much of the technology of the stage. For historical accuracy in costume and scenery, I have never seen anything comparable. An artistic nicety and scrupulousness extends itself to the most inconsidered trifles in which so much of illusion consists, and which commonly are so bungled as to draw attention instead of evading it by an absorption in the universal.

If I had known that I was going to London, I should have been extremely pleased to have made the acquaintance of Ruskin. But my journey thither was sudden and flighty, and I saw nobody except Hogarth, Turner, and Rembrandt. Hogarth's *Marriage à la Mode* and Rembrandt's *Jacob's Dream*, at Dulwich College, gave me invaluable suggestions.

It will not be long now, I hope, before I see you at Elmwood; for you must make me a visit as soon as I get warm in my study again. It is all *Berg ab* now, and I shall ere long feel the swing of our Atlantic once more. The very thought revives me. We seaboard fellows cannot live long without snuffing salt water. Let me hear from you in Italy; tell me what you are painting and all about yourself. As soon as I am myself again, I shall try to make my friendship of some worth to you. But always I am your affectionate friend,

                                      J. R. L.

The next gap in the correspondence is one of over a year. I do not remember, and have no record of the time, when he married his second wife, Frances Dunlap; but the revolution she brought about in his life had begun before his friends knew the causes of it. She was one of the rarest and most sympathetic creatures I have ever known. She was the governess of Lowell's daughter, when I first went to stay at Elmwood, and I then felt the charm of her character. She was a sincere Swedenborgian, with the serene faith and spiritual outlook I have generally found to be characteristic of that sect; with a warmth of spiritual sympathy of which I have known few so remarkable instances; a fine and subtle faculty of appreciation, serious and tender, which was to Lowell like an enfolding of the Divine Spirit. The only particular in which the sympathy failed was in the feeling that she had in regard to his humorous poems. She disliked the vein. It was not that she lacked humour or the appreciation of his, but she thought that kind of literature unworthy of him. This she said to me more than once. But, aside from this, she fitted him like the air around him. He had felt the charm of her character before he went to Europe, and had begun to bend to it; but, as he said to me after his marriage, he would make no sign till he had tested by a prolonged absence the solidity of the feeling he had felt growing up. He waited, therefore, till his visit to Germany had satisfied him that it was sympathy, and not propinquity, that lay at the root of his inclination for her, before declaring himself. No married life could be more fortunate in all respects except one—they had no children. But for all that his life required she was to him healing from sorrow and a defence against all trouble, a very spring of life and hope. A letter from Cambridge (May 14, 1857) must have been written in the interval between his return from Germany and this change in his life, for he had begun his work at the university.

. . . I am glad you do not forget me, though I seem so memoryless and ungrateful. I shall be better one of these days, I hope. While my lectures are on my mind I am not myself, and I seem to see all the poetry drying out of me. I droop on my rocks and hear the surge of the living waters, but they will not reach me till some extraordinary springtide, and maybe not then. . . .

When you come, I wish you to come straight here. We can house you for a while [he was then living with his friend, Dr Estes Howe, in Cambridge, Elmwood having been let for a term] at any rate, and the word "board" is hateful to me. Just now there is a sister of Mrs —— here, with the biggest baby that ever was seen. If the nurse were in proportion, the house would have to be greatened. And there is also the biggest (and nicest) young lady from Ohio. So where could I put you at night, unless I hung you up or leaned you up in a corner, like a beau as you are? But the drift of things will go on, and they will float away on it before long, and then there will be a bed, and that will be better. I will let you know when. I shall be jolly and companionable by that time, which I was not when you were here before, for I could think of nothing but the lectures which were before me. Perhaps you were right about it and I have no business here. However, we die at last and go where there are no lectures.

The apple-trees are in blossom, but I have hardly had time to see them. Horse-chestnuts are in leaf, and linnets and robins sing; but there are not so many birds here as at Elmwood--not so many anywhere as there used to be, and I think the cares of life weigh on them so that they can't sing. We have had only a day or two of warm weather yet. Spring seems like an ill-arranged scene at the theatre that hitches and won't slide forward, and we see winter through the gaps. Bring May with you when you come—remember that. Tell me what your plans are, and when you have arranged to come hitherward and when you would rather. . . .

Your affectionate
J. R. L.

In the next letter there are landmarks of our separate journeys in life. Lowell had married Miss Dunlap; we had made our first excursion to the Adirondacks; the *Atlantic Monthly* had been founded, with Lowell as its editor. I had become his contributor, as he had been mine. In one of my letters after his marriage, I had written to congratulate him, saying that I had already written one letter (probably on hearing of the engagement) and had suppressed it, as too enthusiastic and perhaps boyish.

CAMBRIDGE, 28th October 1857.

MY DEAR STILLMAN,—Thank you for your letters, especially that from the dear old Adirondacks. Though written in pencil, it did my heart more good than my eyes harm, only it made me homesick to be back again

"A chasing the wild-deer and following the roe."

Your last I ought to have answered a week ago; but when I stop payment of letters I do it altogether, and, like a man of honour, allow no favoured creditors.

I should like the article very much. Make it about six or seven pages (print), and at the same time be as lively and as solid as you can. You may have full swing. This is like ordering so many pints of inspiration, eh?— as if Castaly were bottled up like Congress water and sent all over the country for sale. Well, never mind, make it as good as you can. Instructive articles should be sweetened as much as possible, for people don't naturally like to learn anything, and prefer taking their information as much as they can in disguise.

Why did you not send me the enthusiastic letter you say you suppressed? I should have been delighted with it. For God's sake, don't let your enthusiasm go! it is your good genius. When we have once lost it, we would give all the barren rest of our lives to get back but a day of it. Your letter would have hit in the white, too, for I am as happy as I can be, and thank God continually. I have known and honoured my wife for years, but I find some new good in her daily. So you may be as warm as you like in your congratulations. . . .

Affectionately yours,

J. R. LOWELL.

I think it was in the summer of the next year that I went to Cambridge to live, and was thenceforward mainly divided in my occupations between the Adirondacks and the vicinity of "the Oaks" at Waverley until I went to Europe, in the autumn of 1859. Each summer we made an excursion into the Adirondacks, and formed the club which took its name from that region. Under the circumstances, few letters passed between us, for we were not long without seeing each other until I went abroad. Lowell was indeed very happy in his married life, and amongst the pictures Memory will keep on her tablet for me, till Death passes his sponge over it once for all, is one of his wife lying in a long chair under the trees at Dr Howe's, when the sun was getting cool, and laughing with her low, musical laugh at a contest in punning between Lowell and myself, *haud passibus æquis*, but in which he found enough to provoke his wit to activity; her almost Oriental eyes twinkling with fun, half closed and flashing from one to the other of us; her low, sweet forehead, wide between the temples; mouth wreathing with humour; and the whole frame, lithe and fragile, laughing with her eyes at his extravagant and rollicking word-play. One would hardly have said that she was a beautiful woman, but fascinating she was in the happiest sense of the word, with all the fascination of pure and perfect womanhood and perfect happiness.

In those days the boy was still riotous in Lowell; and, until the war came, with its heartbreaking for him and his, and he entered into the larger sphere of public affairs, the escapades of his overflowing and juvenile vitality were irrepressible. In the Adirondacks he cast off all dignity, was one of the best and most devoted shots with the rifle, but proposed to introduce, by regulation, archery for our deerhunting. He was the life of the company, always running over with fun and contrivance of merriment. I remember once, coming home from Boston with those members of the Saturday Club who lived in Cambridge—Agassiz, Howe, Holmes, Lowell, and others, that in the midst of a grave discussion between Agassiz and himself upon the authority of the Scriptures, Lowell, passing through the exit from the college grounds, vaulted suddenly on one of the great stone columns, clapped his hands to his sides, gave a lusty cockcrow, and hopped down again to pursue the argument, insisting on the admission of the Psalms amongst the inspired books. Nothing human was foreign to his sympathies. He knew that I really loved him and was grateful for it; and, though I continually offended his sense of fitness and decorum, doing things wanting in tact and refinement, in sheer and green, if belated, boyishness and want of judgment, he never took offence, but treated me as a younger brother; for he understood my feeling for him, uncouth as were its forms at times; and his benevolence towards me never faltered, though the diverging circumstances of our lives carried us farther and farther apart. His bitter griefs and bereavements during and following our war, his troubles, personal and patriotic, his absorption later in official duties, the accumulating burdens which would have crushed the energies of a smaller man, left his serenity undisturbed; even the disgusting attacks of the Irishry and the politicians, on account of his action in England, only raised a philosophic sarcasm. He was so much "greater than anything he ever did" that I would rather every line he ever wrote were blotted from my memory than that I should forget the days I spent at

Elmwood, or those we spent in the greenwood of the Adirondacks; but one and the other locality, like all those in which I knew him, are forever lonely and desolate to me.

The latest word I have from him was written from the Legation in London, in answer to one inquiring if he had received a bit of Albanian work I had sent him from Montenegro, a new tip to the sheath of a yataghan of some rare and early Albanian silver work, which I had sent him before, but which then lacked its original tip. It is dated 7th of March 1882.

. . . Yes, my dear Stillman, the tip of the sheath arrived safely, and is thought very pretty, although it does not come up to the old work, and could not fairly be called on for such a feat in practical æsthetics. We like it.

You have learned to be satirical in the neighbourhood of the Aristophanic Theatre, but I shake off your sarcasms, not as the lion, but as the duck the dewdrop from his back. I may fairly answer in the Gospel words, "silver and gold have I none," for I am so near my wit's end that I have neither speech nor silence, or feel so, at least. [I had written to ask him to exchange some of his golden silence for a little silver speech.]

But I had enough sentiment left to be a good deal upset by the story of your murder [a telegram from Cettinje had announced that I had been decapitated in Albania], though I did not believe it. I hate the electric telegraph worse than ever.

L

If you come across an ancient statue, send it me by post, and I will pay you in the metal with so much of which you credit me. Mrs Lowell sends her kindest regards, and I remain
    Affectionately always yours,
        J. R. LOWELL.

The handwriting begins to show age—it is tremulous, and the letters are writ large. Death only, if even death, could extinguish the kindly thought, the fine sense of humour, the affectionate fidelity to the past and its ties; nothing had changed in him to the last. When last I saw him, shortly before his recall from London, he certainly showed the signs of age, but I think less than I; the kindly caress in his voice, the flash of humour in his eye, the masterhood in his port, were there as I had known them thirty years before. Wrinkles and grey hair were there, and the tremulousness of the hand in writing; but the mind, though sobered by such sorrows as few men bear, was as serene and spiritual as ever. I could imagine that he laboured under his dispensations as a good ship in a storm, burying his head at times under the wave, but rising to it, shaking off the weight, and keeping on.

Sufficient time has gone by since the death of Lowell for the world to begin to form a judgment on the poet, unbiassed by his influence as a man on those around him; but to those who, like myself, lived in unrestrained intimacy with him, this judgment is impossible, and I will not profess it. Yet it seems to me that he stands as the most perfect representative of the American of New England which has appeared—*i.e.*, the American as he resulted from the hereditary qualities of the Mother-country developed under the surroundings in which New England became a nation, and before the influences born in the war of secession had begun to transform it to what it now is. Be it for better or for worse, the United States is not what it was in the days when Lowell grew up, when the struggle between principles and policies was still fierce and the slavery question made men conscious of a moral responsibility in the nation, the sense of which has now, it seems to me, died out. The change may be, as Lowell hoped, and as we will hope, one of growth, one in which the ultimate character is hidden in the process of metamorphosis, and the final form may be what the passionate patriotism of Lowell prefigured it in his Commemoration Ode:

> "O! Beautiful my Country! ours once more,
> Smoothing thy gold of war-dishevelled hair
> O'er such sweet brows as never other wore,
>   And letting thy set lips,
>   Freed from wrath's pale eclipse,
> The rosy edges of their smile lay bare.
> What words divine of lover or of poet
> Could tell our love and make thee know it—
> Among the nations bright beyond compare?"

and if not, then Lowell remains as the best fruit on a tree prematurely blasted. To me, perhaps, in the blindness of a friendship of whose extremity he was completely worthy as well as of what was much better, he seems the shadowing forth, as the type of the *possible* future American, bred from the best of the world's stock, in the largest of the world's pastures, and destined, if the destiny of the world is towards perfection, to justify the faith of Americans in their stock. But this is, perhaps, too far away even for those who read this to be able to say whether I am a true prophet or not; it seems to me that my country is, at any rate, destined to become the greatest state or the greatest failure of all time; and, in the former case, Lowell will be remembered as the first in time of the citizens of its Parnassus. I have known, loved, and even more, reverenced Emerson; have known well Longfellow, Holmes, Bryant, and most of the men who in that moment of our national existence made it eloquent, but Lowell was, I think, the one most completely and largely American.

I doubt if any foreigner to the land, and, perhaps, even the American of the future, could feel the presence in what Lowell has left of a certain crisp naïveté, which suggests his Hosea Biglow rubbed through the university—a freshness which in a curious way suggests to me the bloom on an untouched and scarcely ripe plum, or what to an extreme classicist may seem want of polish, but which is really the New England impatience at convention, and, if you will, the evidence of the stage of unripeness of the national culture of his day (though it was not always present), and which seems to conventional criticism the indication of crudity in the poet. I think it was in him largely due to a feeling that what was best was what was most spontaneous, and that it was to be spoiled, not finished by the retouching, that the poet was to be brought to perfection in the whole, and not by labour over the parts, and by isolated efforts. If, and when, the education was complete the instantaneous work would show it, seemed to me to be his feeling. He said to me once, and this was after his return from Germany, "I must read and study more before I return to production," as if he felt that in the future the mould must be polished and not the casting.

His sense of the beauty of American landscape was intense, more so I am persuaded even than Bryant's, though less in the nature of landscape painting, and more as background for human interest, like a distance of Titian's. The passage from the Vision of Sir Launfall:

> "A single crow from his tree-top bleak
> From his shining feathers shed off the cold sun,"

is to me the best image of the New England winter I have ever read, and the picture of the winter-palace in the same poem, though of a mingled fancy and imagination, like so much of Lowell's poetry, is a study in the marshes of the Charles River meadows at a winter low-tide, with the thermometer at Zero Fahrenheit. And what was in his work the best painted landscape, was, unmistakably, American subject; the bracing winter, the rapid and bursting spring, the Indian summer, are all treated as not even Bryant would or could have treated them. It was enough that a thing was peculiarly American that he should love it with all his heart; not in chauvinistic narrowness of feeling — and no one who knew him in England could doubt that — but in the passionate preference for his childhood's surroundings, which was willing to see in the crudeness of the New England landscape, with its rail fences and its white-painted farmhouses and its utilitarian uniformity, the bare canvasses on which his fancy painted the memories of boyhood, and in which all that was most tender in the past, of mother and son, of wife and husband, of the graves where he laid his first-born, and—

"That blinding anguish of forsaken clay"

which was his first bereavement—every form and phase of all that was material around him was in this wise mixed with the purest passions human nature is capable of. Through all the home-poems Lowell has left runs this golden thread of sunshine from the sun which shone in the days of a pure and exalted youth, whose dreams and memories are better and dearer than the realities of the most prosperous later life. In the warmth of this light all Lowell's imagery is more or less steeped, and the landscape which the landscape painter turns from as beyond pictures, was the ever-beautiful world in which Lowell lived. It may be the fancy of one to whom the man was dear as woman, but to me the passionate purity of Lowell's life glows in his poetry; and this, as well as other associations which are beyond imparting, blind the critic in me.

> "What words divine of lover or of poet
> Could tell our love and make thee know it?"

THE DECAY OF ART

THAT no grave inquiry into the causes of the decline in art in modern times should have taken place at a time when scientific investigation ranges over every branch of human cognitions, is only to be explained by the conviction held even in highly organised political communities, that art in general has no especial function in a national life, and may be left out of the curriculum of the citizen of the world and he be none the worse citizen for it, or that art is merely the representation of nature's facts and so simply the accessory to science, and as such comprehended in it. But we have the unquestionable fact that every nation which has progressed beyond the most primitive barbarism, has, before beginning that phase of civilisation which is characterised mainly by the accumulation of superfluities, been most intensely interested in and largely influenced by not only poetry and music, but that process of beautifying one's self and surroundings which is the vital principle of art. "Ornament was before dress," and the daily lives of innumerable artists prove that a man may be content with deprivation of a serious character and be happy even in unrecompensed devotion to art; the ambition of life satisfied with victories that have no victims, and gains that make no one the poorer. It is a question philosophy may well take up in earnest: how far the strain of modern life, the inordinate inequalities in society, and the extravagance of large classes of it, might be modified by restoring the arts, as far as cultivation can accomplish it, to the influence they held in the life of Greece in 500 to 400 B.C., and more or less as long as the Greeks remained free. It is perfectly true that art has seen some of its best phases coinciding with a debauched social condition and a degraded national life; but, in these cases, the art itself became rapidly debauched and formal, as did religion; but no art ever originated in debauchery or, in its noblest alliances, long survived a healthy intellectual activity, more or less accompanied by moral soundness. In the best art of a demoralised people there are visible the symptoms of decomposition—moral gangrene.

That art is, and always has been, in a sense, the exponent of the real character of a nation is a fact noted by philosophers and writers on art for a long time. That if the life shapes the art, there must be in some degree a counter-influence of the art over the life, seems to be settled by the laws of cause and effect, as well as that that influence might, under favourable circumstances, prove analogous to that of literature, and equally important in its cultivation. What is certain is, that in our veritable life, the purely mental existence, the elements which comprise the various forms of pleasure are, the normal activity of the intellectual powers, and the perception of beauty.

The question which arises, and which it is rash for any man to offer a reply to, is this: Has modern life become so differentiated from that of the early stages of human existence that the influence of beauty and the dependent influence of art become no longer essential to the healthful progress of the human intellect? And beyond this lies a question to which Plato gives an unhesitating answer: Whether beauty be not the chief witness to man's immortality?—a motive of greater moment, if such a thing could be shown, than his present content.

I indicate this scope of a possible inquiry partly to show its possible importance, and partly to indicate the particular branch of it which I wish now to examine. Why have the arts of design steadily and everywhere fallen off in excellence and influence in modern times? On the philosophical side it would be easy to answer that it was due to the materialism of the modern life; but this, while perfectly true, is still a remote cause, because we have, in individual cases, found gross materialism in the artist not inconsistent with grandeur and great power in his art. A certain analogy between religion and art is found in the relation of both to modern scientific research. The spirit of exact inquiry, and the limitation of our cognitions to material and demonstrable phenomena, is waging war on that entire range

THE DECAY OF ART 171

of spiritual faculties, perceptions, emotions, on which all religious systems have been founded and in which lie the true roots of art. Is the decay of art due to the same tendencies? If yes, is it not clear that the official and collective efforts to restore art are as futile for this restoration as those of state churches to reform our morality? Nevertheless, there is to most minds, even scientific, an indefinable and inevitable recognition of something, beyond and above, which has not fallen under these attacks and which we must find out.

But science and nature cannot go wrong. In the light of positive knowledge and physical demonstration we cannot regret beliefs whose bases are disproved. It is useless to shut out light. If we must face the destruction of the ideal, let us accept the inevitable with at least the courage of the ignorant and fanatic, and not waste strength in defence of delusions. Yet there is, perhaps, more danger in the too hasty deduction of truth from phenomena than in delaying our adhesions to what seem well-proved facts. We have always a right to wait, and, remembering past revolutions of thought, to question finality in human discovery; while admitting, as an abstract question, that exact science must lead ultimately to final truth. And convinced of this, I still believe in Religion, and, as I am not without hope that Science may some day show us immortality, and that matter is not all, so I trust that we shall find even in the Actual the proof that the Ideal is something better and nobler than the Actual's accidental results, and that Art is no more bound to follow Nature than Religion to serve Science.

I have no intention here to attack this complicated and contested question, and have thus far approached it only to show on what ground and by what analogies, amongst others, the legitimacy and supremacy of subjective or ideal art can be supported. For at present we have to deal with two distinct forms of so-called art, of which the elder and true form, the subjective, is an art of expression, whereof the vital quality is that it shall convey, not the facts and actual phenomena which constitute the anatomy of nature, but the emotions and impressions of the artist, in which all the visible forms are but the symbols of language in which the artist, without any restriction of realistic fidelity, shall show forth what he considers artistic truth or ideal beauty in any of its related forms of positive or negative. The other form, objective, or realistic art, which is entirely the development of the naturalistic spirit, depends, for its relative value and standing, upon the fidelity which it shows to natural phenomena—it is the art, if it be art, of facts and physics, of the anatomist, the geologist, the botanist, and the portraitist. The methods, the appeals, the faculties, and the results of these two are antithetical — they are related as science and poetry, or, to use a less generally comprehensible, but by genuine art students perfectly understood, comparison, as Truth and Fact; one free with all the liberty of the

THE DECAY OF ART

imaginative life, and the other bound in obedience to the accidents of nature. It is the former of these which has fallen into decay and which is the subject of our inquiry. But *en passant*, I will call attention to the fact which explains itself, that the noblest technique has arisen in the art of expression, and that, for certain forms of it, we have to seek the highest in antique or Renaissance art.

The realistic or naturalistic art is a purely modern conception. It had been long foreshadowed by a literary movement, whereby the great intellectual interest has gradually shifted from the epic to the pictures of society and humanity in the modern novel. The popular literature had its intermediate phase of romanticism like art, and has finally, like it again, settled down to questions of realism; but, as poetry preceded art by unknown centuries, so its ultimate development into the realism, which seems the chief interest of the modern intellect, long preceded the corresponding development of art.

The parallel offers interesting study for thinkers on all the forms of thought-development, but what is of especial interest from the point of view which it is my intention to take, is the important bearing it ought to have on the questions of art education, in which our society seems to hold so high but so unintelligent an interest. The question at issue is practical: I am persuaded that a complete explanation of the reason of this decay would ultimately lead, firstly, to a true understanding of the proper and unique value of the arts of design and visible appeal; and, secondly, to a measurable restoration to their true and productive channels of the energies and appreciation which in other ages gave us an art, compared to which ours is a pigmy.

This decadence can be disputed by no one with the most moderate knowledge of art or feeling for it. It does not consist merely in the sinking of the ideal standard, or the incidental variation of national temperament; it is shown in the most purely technical qualities, as well as the intellectual. There were men who painted contemporaneously with, or immediately after, the great Renaissance painters, whom we scarcely know by name, yet whose work is frequently confounded with that of their great masters merely on account of its technical excellence. Without any intellectual dignity, it shows an executive power and excellence of method which no painter of our time can equal; and, even in work absolutely unassignable to any known painter, we find examples of such a thorough mastery of the material and power of hand as would give any living painter distinct precedence in modern art.

It is no answer to these statements to say that our age does not want what past ages demanded and accepted as the best; that Titian's work would not find purchasers if done to-day; and that no one would go to see the Sistine Chapel if a living painter had painted it—the fact remains that no one to-day can do the work of

Titian even with Titian's doing of it before him, and that no man living can match a study of Michael Angelo for one of his figures, not to speak of his Sistine Chapel.

I will not go back to Greek sculpture, whose supremacy no one contests, but only to that lovely and faithful dream of it which came with the Italian Renaissance in the works of the Pisani, Mino Da Fiesole, Donatello, Michael Angelo, Giovanni da Bologna, all men who had caught the spirit of Greek art however much they faltered and wavered in giving it form, and challenge the eighteenth or nineteenth centuries to show us anything born of the same heaven and earth. Of the great painters of the same epoch of art development we have no more a single peer in the modern schools — Doré for Buonarotti, Makart for Veronese, Munkácsy for Tintoretto, Ingres for Raphael, and Delacroix for Titian.

And, in spite of all this, we pay artists as artists never were paid before, unless by the caprice of some reckless or imperial spendthrift in exceptional cases; munificence becomes extravagance, prodigality, and what we get for its highest prices is Meissonier and Millais; for schools we have the Royal Academy, South Kensington, the École des Beaux Arts, and cruder American imitations; but Meissonier stands at the head of orthodox art in France, as Millais did in England. Nor is it merely a question of national temperament — the countrymen of

Velasquez, of Rubens, of Titian, of Holbein are in no other plight than we; still less is it a question of decaying intellect, as the mental activity of the whole race shows. Neither the multitude of devotees, the intensity of application of the mental capacity, the social encouragement, nor the adequacy of pecuniary reward, is lacking. There are many painters paid as painters never were before in proportion to the art they produce—fêted, courted, knighted and decorated; and the further we go in this road the more is art heartless, mechanical, vain.

The reason is to seek. Science turns her back on the subject, and the universities dismiss art from the category of studies and pass it over mainly to the painters to discourse on, ignoring the psychological law that no mind can be productively analytical and synthetical at the same time; and the artist, being perforce a synthesist, cannot be expected to analyse the art which he is, if a true artist, occupied in building. There is no case, except that of Leonardo da Vinci, where we find high speculative or analytical power combined with great artistic gifts, and this case is precisely the one which proves my proposition, for Da Vinci, even in his art, was a naturalist rather than a poet; he was of a generation in which every form of mental activity and social movement sympathised with art, and especially he had, in extraordinary degree, the mechanical gifts which have so great an importance in technical art, and correspond so closely in their mental position with the great executive faculties of the artist, so that to him painting was the most apparent outlet for his energies. Had he lived in our age he had most certainly been an engineer and mechanician; for, even in the quality of his art, it is the scientific and imitative elements which dominate, while the imaginative and emotional, which, above all, distinguish the great art of all time, are curiously deficient. Of a sincerely devout though questioning mind, his religion led him to art by one tie, while the difficulty of then attaining to social position without high birth and family influence made art almost the only avenue to eminence for men of great intellectual activity, disposed neither to the church nor to the army. And as it was, we see that his art enlisted but a small part of his study, while his note-books in all their precepts point rather to the naturalistic than the artistic side of painting, though not by modern methods.

Therefore it is that when we demand general critical powers, and such analysis of art as is necessary to evolve the laws by which its study must be directed, it is quite useless to look to the artists to serve us. It has, indeed, passed into a common saying that an artist is never a competent critic; but this, like most other popular proverbs, only expresses the vulgar and superficial side of the truth it relates to, the truth being that, while artists are generally illogical and one-sided in their appreciation of any special form of art, there is no possibility of being a competent critic of art without something of that technical training which, when successful in a high degree, makes the artist of distinction. If we could but collect and reduce to system the occasional criticisms and dicta of men like Watts, J. F. Millet, Rossetti, Delacroix, Burne-Jones, Th. Rousseau, etc., we should have a body of precepts and criticisms such as no writer on art has ever given or can ever give us; but the peculiar form of intellectual activity which is needed to put this *corpus inscriptionum* into a logical and consequent form, as a code of art, is not compatible with the artistic intellect. Da Vinci began such a book, but it still remains in the form of notes. No man not practically versed in art to such an extent that he can at least measure the difficulties to be met, and appreciate the skill that has overcome them; whose eye is not trained by practice in drawing so that he may judge discriminatingly of the forms before him; and who has not, moreover, made himself thoroughly acquainted with the body of evidence to be collected from the great work of the old schools; who does not know, in fact, both nature and art by intimate and special study—can have any valid authority in criticism of art in any form. We have a much completer scientific basis for criticism of music than of painting, but no one proposes to write musical criticisms without mastering counterpoint and acquiring some practical and executive knowledge of the elements of music. In art criticism such effrontery is of everyday occurrence.

It is one thing to enumerate abstract principles of criticism, which may be evolved by analogy from well-ascertained parallels in other intellectual studies, and another to apply them in such a way as to give sound, concrete judgments on particular forms of art. Of the former kind of generalisation about art, we have many excellent examples in the writing of men whose opinions on individual works of art are absurdly whimsical and inconsequent. The name of Professor Ruskin will at once be put forward as that of the critic who has best fulfilled all the conditions imposed on the ideal critic, and he would be a rash man who contested his claim to the first place, or his splendid services to modern thought. But, in point of fact, and so far as the claims of the highest art are concerned, he has simply retarded their recognition by basing all his teaching on direct study of nature, and insisting on a realistic basis for art. So far as I know, the best result of practical knowledge of art, applied to the elucidation of the principles of criticisms, is in the works of Mr Hamerton. Sir Joshua Reynolds has left us a series of lectures and some fragmentary notes which are of great value in the technical education of the artist, but which in nowise attempt any explanation of the principles of art from the logical side, or trench on its philosophy.

The German philosophers have, on the other hand, contributed much valuable material to the study of that philosophy, and we owe to them such basis for its development as we possess; though, in every attempt to apply their fundamental principles to education or concrete criticism, they fail through want of catholicity of appreciation. We owe to them the clear statement of the fundamental distinction between the elements which constitute the dualism of art, the *objective* and *subjective*, as well as the formulation of the science of the æsthetic. Baumgarten, to whom the honour of having projected this science belongs, defines it as "the theory of the liberal arts, inferior to gnoseology, the art of beautiful thought, . . . the science of sense cognition." But the value of this very valid advance in art philosophy was not realised by Baumgarten, because the nomenclature of art was, as it still is, in no state to supply the terms of the logical discussion. There was no definition of an art which constituted a definite distinction from a science. What was an art at one time became a science later, and the confusion common to his day betrayed him into an inconsistency which now makes his essay more or less absurd. But his definition of æsthetics as the science of the beautiful remains to us. We are still too much encumbered by the nomenclature which betrayed him, and under which any definite assertion may be met by another which pre-supposes an entirely different conception of art. We have the fine arts, the polite arts, the useful arts; the art which is simply skill in doing anything, equivalent to the Greek τέχνη — the secret of doing anything, the rule for which becomes matter of science when established. It may be a trick or it may be a Greek sculpture that engages us, and we may have, to discuss it, masters of arts who know no art. An artist may be a Titian, a Beethoven, an actor, a dancer, a singer, a juggler, a pickpocket; the tailor, the milliner, any workman, may be "quite an artist in his way." How can we define art or the artist? We must avail ourselves of that natural process of differentiation in terminology which is continually going on, and according to which the leading claimants to the general rank of artist are distinguished by their peculiar appellations. A composer is taken to mean the writer of music, a poet the writer of verse, a musician the performer of music, and the performer of plays an actor; even the sculptor has a range of work so definite and distinct that, though no one questions the quality of his art, he is generally known as a sculptor rather than by the wider term, and so a prevailing (which might well be made authoritative) acceptation of the words *art* and *artist*, when in nowise qualified, implies the arts of design and those who follow them. Even in the arts of design a common and, perhaps, unconscious distinction is put forward of greater or less, one painter being known as a true artist, and another only as an unintelligent imitator or copyist. This custom does not consider photography an art or a photographer an artist, and as the work of a painter approaches the quality of photography we recognise that it recedes from art.

I believe this development of a more definite terminology to be in accordance with the true philosophy of art, and that it points to the severe definition of the Artist as the Creator.

> "The artist saw his statue of the soul
> Was perfect; so with one regretful stroke
> The earthen model into fragments broke,
> And without her the impoverished seasons roll."

The supreme artist is the idealist, and the imitator of nature is the artist only in a lower and secondary sense, and this distinction has become a differentiated conclusion in general English speech and thought. Baumgarten's æsthetics, the science of the beautiful, is, therefore, the science of art in its restricted sense of design; and design, in its severe and only logical sense, is the creation (from the material stored in the imagination) of a visible ideal. We can in nowise admit to a parity with the idealist any realist, no matter how triumphant. The question is not one of comparison, but of contrast; the distinction is radical; it is that between poetry and science, the imagination and simple vision. Extreme illustrations will be found in J. F. Millet and Meissonier, each magnificent examples of the two classes of minds, each successful in its aim, and each, alas! a type as well of the estimation in which modern society hold them:

Millet, the most subtle and masterly example of the pure Greek method of approaching art, dying in comparative poverty and neglect; and Meissonier, the extreme manifestation of the purely modern spirit, realism reduced to its last expression, wealthy and idolised, the object of the shallow enthusiasms of a society that hardly cares to study what it admires. It is impossible, on any sound theory of art, to put together work so radically, as well as superficially, distinct—no rules of criticism or precept of schools will embrace both.

To contribute ever so little to the clear setting forth of those cardinal distinctions, which must underlie all productive criticism and so aid in forming a sound theory of art education, it is necessary to go back to the radical distinctions between these two kinds of art, and to make it impossible to confound the paths of approach. It may be possible to walk alternately in both if it were desirable, but it ought not to be possible to confound them or mistake one for the other.

Professor Ruskin, with all his power and subtlety of thought (and I regard the second volume of "Modern Painters" the most pregnant contribution of our generation to a sound æsthetic literature), has, *me judice*, missed the reforms he had at heart by his rejection in theory and practice of the fundamental distinction of objective and subjective, and by his insistence on rigid realisation of nature as a method of art education. That element in art which makes it such is not its fidelity to nature but its personality;

the way in which the artist arranges, subordinates, harmonises the material which he borrows or invents; in the majesty or sweetness of his composition, the harmony and pathos or splendour of his colour; all those things which in poetry, in music, give rank as poet or musician. The law is the same in all the arts; it is always the subjective element which determines the place of the artist. In music and in poetry there is no room for confusion on this subject; and, to one who will reflect, it is no less clear that the whole power of painting over the emotions is due to qualities which are entirely independent of any question of representation of natural objects. Even is it true that the glow of sunset and the gloom of twilight owe their fascination and the power they have over the artist mainly to the liberty they give to escape from the facts of nature, from the domination of an inflexible materialism. If painting owed its power to the representation of nature, the noonday should have more value to the painter than the evening, which everybody knows is not the fact, and as twilight, as phenomenon, has no more value or rarity than daylight, it appears that the value it has is in a certain correspondence with moods of the mind more grateful and potent than the perception of facts. This points to a metaphysical investigation, in which I do not enter farther than to state my conclusion that twilight and others of the greater phases of nature, which have a special artistic appeal, owe it, not to the fact that they are forms of phenomena, but to the relation between them and certain moods inherent in the human mind—*i.e.*, to their subjectivity, just as, in a larger way, physical beauty owes its fascination, not to its being a fact, but to its accord with certain unexplained chords of human emotion.

Art is simply the harmonic expression of human emotion. Where there is no emotion there is no art, except in that secondary sense which has been pointed out, and which relates to the primary as the letter to the spirit. Nature furnishes symbols but no language. The arts which are the legitimate daughters of the muse are, dancing, music, poetry, sculpture and painting—so in the order of their birth; if organic nature has been called in to nurse the latter more openly than the former, the parentage is nowise changed. The entire quality of all art is misrepresented and misunderstood by any other hypothesis. The law which controls the poem or symphony is the same which guides the pencil or chisel of the true artist.

That all great art—be it of school or individual —obeys this law, is capable of proof. It is only, moreover, as part of human life and motive that it has any claim to the consideration we give it. If, as I believe to be beyond doubt, the art impulse is the first of the humanities in the race as in the child, then, in the highest conception of life, is it equally true that art is, for the happiness of the race, a necessity, and its wise fostering a part of true political economy, of which human happiness is the legitimate end. Every human being, in proportion as the child-like nature survives in him, is dependent on art for his happiness, and the happiest are those to whom art has longest kept its realities.

This, in most men's experience of their kind, is a commonplace, interpret it as we may; but in modern culture it is ignored in a twofold and singular manner. Art is commonly held a too trivial branch of study for adult intellects; or, where provision is made for its culture, we ignore the facts that its roots are entirely in the emotional—*i.e.*, subjective or poetic—*i.e.*, creative (ποιέω, I make) faculties, and not at all in the objective or scientific, which latter when cultivated *per se* are not only antipathetic but destructive to art. The scientist is the natural enemy of art in every form, as the scientific tendency is to the emotional, which is the indispensable aliment of art.

All the great schools of painting and sculpture have been purely subjective in their origin and development, and all have been in the former purely decorative; abstract or subjective forms of decoration in all cases preceding imitative or naturalistic—an unmistakable indication that the earliest pictorial impulse was creative and not imitative. The schools grew by the sapient accumulation of sound tradition and the development of the ideal of beauty, always regarded originally as superhuman. All grew up as schools of music still grow, and to all these came a time when they began to lean on nature-study and so on realism and scientific methods of looking at nature, in which were the causes of decay. No great school ever was founded on the direct or objective study of nature, nor, at its prime, was any school ever guilty of it; but the moment the subjective method which was its life gave way to the objective or scientific method, the art began to go down. The moment of completest triumph, in which art seemed to have added to its proper charm that of the realistic fidelity which wins the universal applause, was that in which decline began. This was the epoch of Praxiteles and Scopas, of Titian and Raphael; and when, finally, at Bologna, the academy model took the place of the ideal, there was no longer any hope of any school of art.

The reason for this is not difficult to state. The genuine creative art or ideal art is only possible where there is full liberty to embody distinct and homogeneous conceptions which, so far as the word can be properly applied to human work, are creations; and here the mental conception must be so clear in the mind of the artist that it serves the mental vision as the type of which the work of art is the visible embodiment. In all great design this vital quality is most clearly evident; but when constant and concurrent reference to the model is kept up this is not possible, and the slightest indication of the model shown in design is immediately destructive of this supreme quality of art. The great artists of past ages have left us no specific declaration in words of their recognition of this law, but the internal evidence in their works is abundant. There can be no doubt that the Greek sculptors never worked directly from nature, but from an intimate knowledge, in which the perfectly-trained eye co-operated with the habit of working from an ideal developed through a subtle sense of the beautiful in form, whereof the complete realisation was no more to be found in any visible natural type then than now. We know the same to be true of Michael Angelo; and in all the work of the great painters of the Italian schools, we find constant and unmistakable indications that they did not work before nature. Of the greatest of living idealists, and, in the noble sense of art, the highest modern example of the combination of its greatest qualities, G. F. Watts, we have the distinct and invariable rule never to work from the model in any ideal (*i.e.*, other than portrait) work.

Not only is this the immutable law of all great art, but I maintain that the scientific study of nature, whether as anatomy, geology, or botany, is obnoxious in a high degree to the development of the great qualities of design. Beauty, which is the loftiest of all the attributes of art, is purely a visible and therefore superficial quality. To know the structure of the human body, to be able to create the bones and their articulations, the muscles and their insertions, is to confuse the ideal perception with things which are not of vision but of another kind of knowledge. We know that the Greeks had no knowledge of anatomy or of the use of the muscular system; that they regarded the strength of the body as in the bones to which the muscles were merely protecting cushions. We can see in Michael Angelo the ostentation of the anatomist showing through the perception of the ideal, and marring it in spite of his immense and unapproached imaginative power, and in the lesser men of the school of Raphael can follow the decadence that came from this pride of knowledge. But, even then, the habit of direct study of the subject from nature, or the attempt to so represent the scene that it should appear an actuality—an historical transcript of the scene—was unknown.

The Dutch painters, though they sought the most trivial details in nature, never became entirely objective in their work, and only approximately in still life. In their landscape and sea pieces the colouring and rendering of detail are purely conventional, and aim, not at reproducing the colour of nature, but at giving harmonies in various keys of grey colour, and at expressing the quality of natural objects by peculiarities of execution which are not at all inspired directly by, or true to, the detail of nature.

Down to the last of the great schools, that of Rembrandt, Teniers and Rubens, the deference to nature, except in portraiture, never went further than to make sketches from nature, in which the essential qualities were recorded in such a way as to leave the artist at full liberty to modify in his painting either tone or form to suit his individual feeling. Hobbema and Ruysdael, who, of all the Dutch painters, came nearest to the minor facts of nature, clearly never painted from her directly or used her otherwise than as a vehicle for their ideals of composition and colour.

That true and delightful school of English landscapists which began with Girtin, was completely subjective in its methods and in its appeals, and is the only collective movement in English art which deserves the name of a distinctive school. So far as it had any artistic progenitors, it was due to the influence of Claude, Poussin, and the Dutch landscapists, but with a robust individuality and fresh poetic feeling which no other landscape had ever shown, a near and intimate inspiration from the larger qualities of unsophisticated nature, which made it more poetic than any prior school of landscape had been. Turner, who was its greatest master, and who attained the highest expression of subjective art of his time— possibly of all time—was in no period of his career a student of nature in the modern acceptation of that term. No painter ever so nonchalantly defied all the actualities, or took such startling liberties with the broader verities of landscape as he. It was not merely topography that he upset and the mountains that he marshalled about, but he outdid Joshua in the liberties he took with the sun and moon. If he ever realised a tint of actual nature, it was simply because in his chromatic scale it happened to hit the note he wanted. An audacious defiance of facts was not enough; he set at nought the larger laws, and his colour from the beginning to the end of his career was a constantly widening and complicating scheme of chromatic harmonies as perfectly subjective as a symphony. Light, space, colour; that subtle synthesis of lines and forms which his most influential master Claude taught him and which we call composition; modulation of tint which never left a vacant space in any portion of his work; orchestration as complex, as masterly, as ever musician mastered—these were what he sought; and if the forms of nature and her combinations furnished him with the elements of his work, he accepted them certainly, but with the liberty which belongs to one to whom nature is a useful servant, not an imperious mistress.

When the full force of the poetic tendency which produced this school of English landscape-painters was broken by the rise and fascination of nature-painting, I do not know. The work was done ere Turner died; and with him, Linnell, S. Palmer, and some minor men of the same general tendency, the school disappeared. It died out as the Greek and the Italian schools had died, from a method of study initiated by portraiture and the sudden recognition of an interest in nature never felt before by the general mind. The Dutch painters had long held a controlling influence over the dilettanti of England, as painters whose work could be partially understood by men who had no knowledge of art—a copper kettle of Ostade or Teniers gave more real pleasure to the average buyer of pictures than a Madonna of Raphael or Botticelli, though the Dutchman only did such things as *tours de force*, and to show his skill. His system of study was still more subjective than objective; but when the modern landscape and genre painter brought into painting a clear unconventional way of seeing nature, and uncompromising fidelity in rendering facts requiring neither knowledge of, nor feeling for, art in its public, or poetic insight in its painter, it developed intellectual indolence in the latter and flattered the ignorance and conceit of the former, and brought into existence what is commonly supposed to be a rational art, but which is, in reality, the negation of art.

There is one interesting phenomenon that is connected with this arrival of a school of art at its climax and its subsequent rapid decay, which deserves explanation. In the subjective method, or working "out of one's head," as the common expression goes, the mind forms certain conventional modes of expression, and follows these with an increasing approach to fidelity until the art reaches that point which we take for the acme, so near to perfection is it when seen from our lower plane. Then, whether by law or by a recurring chance, the artist finds his way to realisation, the more or less literal reproduction of what nature puts before him—generally, I believe, through intellectual indolence; perhaps more or less through methods induced by portraiture, and persisted in on account of the charm which all men have felt who ever made a faithful study from nature, and which appeals to new sources of enjoyment. In the satisfaction due to successful and complete imitation lies a triumph far more facile than those of the ideal method, and which appeals to that general appreciation to which few men are great enough to be indifferent; for the artist above most men craves the appreciation of his fellow-men. This change seems to have occurred generally, if not invariably, at the close of long periods of purely artistic activity, and after rapid increase of civic and individual prosperity, when the comparatively uneducated taste of the community at large was the court to which the artist appealed. Then, with this lowered standard and sacrifice of·the ideal, nature became the mistress of the school, and the old way and the old insight departed. Art was no longer expression, poetry, but a representation, a simulation, more or less earnest, of an actuality: first, history, sacred or profane or commonplace; and so in time came genre, story-painting, etc., etc., with much pride in rendering of stuffs and illusions, of light and shade, descending to a kind of intelligent photography.

And so it happens that in our time we have only sporadic cases of the true method of the study of art, and that beside them occurs a form of art which was never known in the days of the ideal art—viz., the strictly historical, of which Ford Madox Brown was in England the most conspicuous example, and of which much might be said, but by me at present only that it relates to the art of the ideal, the supreme art whose loss we deplore, as history does to poetry and music.

That the inspiration is not extinct, we have proof in our own days, in France, in Delacroix, J. F. Millet—in intellectual ability quite the peers of the men of the great schools—in America, in Allston, and in England, in Watts, Burne-Jones, Rossetti: each of the great type, eminent, distinct, entirely individual, but each, unfortunately, compelled to work out his results alone, groping for the true method by the aid of the light remaining to us in the works of the great masters of the Greek and Italian schools, but with no leading or following of their own time.*

Since the days of the great Renaissance masters, no man has comprehended so fully and applied so successfully the spirit of Greek art as Watts, and none has caught so perfectly that of the Renaissance as Burne-Jones. Rossetti, like Turner, stood alone. He even less resembled all his predecessors, and has been followed by no disciples. For felicity of imaginative design, nothing in art surpasses some of the work of his youth — such drawings, for instance, as his *Cassandra*, *Hamlet*, and the *Magdalen's First Sight of Christ*; or, in chromatic brilliancy and weird harmony, some of the water-colour drawings, all drawn to the minutest details from imaginative vision. What

---

* It is in my personal knowledge that Mr Watts has said that he would have been a better painter if he had had the advantage of a training in youth in Titian's studio, instead of arriving late by his own research at the proper methods of execution.

he might have done for art, had his life and health been spared, we can only conjecture; but what he has left is a page of art history, brilliant, indeed, but even more suggestive of what might have been. If, again, we demand technical "mastery," the knowledge of the processes which are required in art production, that which was the qualification to become a teacher in the great Italian schools, there is only, in England, W. B. Richmond, competent to do in a workmanlike manner any work set before him, without which competence no man can be called a "master."

The public of to-day prefers a form of art which shall require no previous study, and make no appeal to faculties beyond keen optics. It likes work studded with fine bits of realism and whose story lies on the surface. A thoroughly realistic perception of natural colour (not so common a gift, however, as the public imagines) and a masterly execution are sufficient to secure the painter's position. Imagination and imaginative fusion, and the sense of ideal beauty which make what is commonly called "high art" and may be called *true art*, are no longer necessary to place the artist in the position of authority which would give rise to a school. The great schools of art were founded in the search for these supreme qualities. The artists went into them as students of music now go in youth to study while the hand and thought are flexible — Titian and Michael Angelo at eight and ten years of age—and the whole course of study was one which widened and deepened the intellectual nature in the direction of art. This early entry into the school, invariable in the practice of the great schools, is, to my opinion, the condition *sine qua non* of any mastery in painting and sculpture as in music, or in the acquisition of any other language. Expression must be unconscious to be supreme. The minor men were caught up by the power and influence of the masters' minds into the majesty of the school, and the masters quickened and stimulated each other's genius. The morbid vanity of individualism, tending to eccentricity, did not carry men out of the sound traditions of their masters, but the true scholars laboured collectively for the attainment of the ideal of their school. Now, *stat nominis umbra*—there is no school. Drawing classes there are, and lessons at so much an hour, but no masters, and therefore no schools. The drawing and painting classes teach technical virtues, and all—classes, painters, and exhibitions, exalt the imitation of nature as the end of art.

The end it is, but in another sense—its grave. To know nature and employ her terms for the expression of the artist's ideal, is a widely different thing from the imitation of her forms and facts. The former is an education, it wakens a kinship to all great thought and all great thinkers; the latter narrows and dwarfs the intellect and exterminates the imagination. So long as the modern thinker only accepts realism and nature-reproduction as art, art education must remain a shallow and unimportant branch of modern in-

tellectual development, and art stay where it is—
the servant of all fashions and fancies, huckster
of stuffs and bric-a-brac, *tableaux vivants* and still
life, archæological restorations and mediæval *poses
plastiques*—anything and everything but essential
truth and ideal beauty. If this is to be the conclusion of the education on which we are concentrating our forces, it is hardly necessary to say
that the play is not worth the candle.

THE REVIVAL OF ART

In one of his most important and suggestive essays, that on Culture, Emerson has the following sentence: "Whilst all the world is in pursuit of power, and of wealth as a means of power, culture corrects the theory of success." No man was better qualified to estimate the qualities and value of culture by his own experience, or to judge of the dignity or the reverse, of success, by the daily spectacle all round him of the most successful pursuit of power and wealth that any society has ever afforded—viz., that in the great commonwealth of the American Republic. He stood at the head of its culture; and, in a country where intellect has only to choose the path to power and accept the sacrifices and compensations demanded to acquire it, he remained indifferent to it and the means to it, died poor and indifferent to politics and other distinction than that his culture gave him. Emerson has often been called the American Plato, and amongst the mental qualities which justify the claim was the curious insensibility to the attractions of art. Plato had no place in his community for the artist; Emerson, in a time and state of society in which nature has brought art nearer to the daily life of men, through the invention of landscape, photography, etc., etc., remained all his life insensible in a remarkable degree to contemporary art. He felt *nature* as the ancient Greeks seem to have felt her, apart from the human subjective uses of her; and this trait, in the mental conformation of a man so typical of the race which seems to be evolving the type of civilisation for the next phase of human development, is a phenomenon which invites study. We talk a great deal about art, and spend a great deal of time and money on it, but it is a serious question if art has any more hold on the modern mind, or has any more share in modern culture than alchemy or astrology. And when I say that it is a serious question, I mean not only that it is one that may have serious import, but that it may be seriously held in the negative as well as positive, and seriously debated. But to debate it, to maintain either the negative or the positive, it is necessary to understand with precision what art means; and if, in the grave deliberations the subject may call up, it should be discovered that it is a necessary part of modern culture, this understanding must be applied to the system of education devoted to it.

I do not recognise the ignorant and substantially superstitious respect, often amounting to reverence, for the artist, and begetting an impulsive patronage of him, as implying or leading to a knowledge of art—it is a feeling strong in proportion to the ignorance of art in the individual, and is a phenomenon of the religious nature, a shadow of the lingering reverence for a creator, and, as given to art, is strongest in weak minds. It is that which impels so many to think they must "do something for art"; leads to some intelligent, but more unintelligent patronage of it by individuals, schemes of art schools and art education by communities, in which the patronage of artists and fostering of art are confounded—sometimes identified, sometimes mistaken, the one for the other, to the injury of both. The artist is no more entitled to respect or charity, much less to reverence, than any other brain worker; that he excites our wonder by feats of legerdemain, *tours de force*, tricks of the brush, or audacities of technique is due purely to our ignorance, and counts for the artisan, not for the artist; in true art the means are so completely subordinated to the end that they are not, and ought not to be, noticed. Nor is fidelity to nature any more the standard to which we should bring our critical measures to be tried; the photograph is truer to nature than any art can be, and is yet the very antipodes of art. Yet, these are the qualities which determine the exhibition success, the fame and fortune of the artist; and, by the theory of success, determine the nature of the education of the artist so far as the public has anything to do with it. The dominant virtues in the general estimation and in the success of the Royal Academy exhibitions are, first, clever brush work; and second, fidelity to the facts of nature. And with these ideals in view, the education in art of our public, and to a greater or less extent of our artist, is shaped. If the general public is content, it is an argument to strengthen the case of those who maintain that the uses of art are matters of the past, and that of its finer qualities, as of its true methods, we are in equal ignorance and indifference.

And yet we have under our eyes, and held up to our admiration, the products of the two great schools of the past, the Greek and the Italian Renaissance, which all thoughtful students of art recognise as beyond modern rivalries; with the contemporary Japanese, in which, with an antipodal difference of motive and temperament, the fundamental system is the same, and the success due to the same processes of thought and work as those of the Greek and Italian schools. These processes are absolutely antagonistic to those of the modern European schools without exception, the difference between the latter being rather one of processes and handiwork than in conception of the purposes of art, or more or less vital affinity with the essential motives of art, in the correct theory of it. The English school is, with very few but most notable exceptions, only an aggregation of more or less clever amateurs; the German, a mistaken philosophical worship of the mass of matter we call the world, and humanity, without a trace of imagination or spirituality; and the French, of the moment, while technically at the head of modern art, is but the apotheosis of brush work and the speculum of the surface of things, as devoid of vitality, as cold and sterile as the surface of the moon. It is useless to call up men like Millet, Th. Rousseau, and two or three more: they are voted out of the scheme of to-day, and form no part of the French system any more than Watts, Burne-Jones, and Rossetti of the English. These are survivals of a condition of the human intellect which, though once normal, has ceased to be so.

The steady degradation of art, almost without distinction of form, with only rare and isolated recurrences of the true spirit, from the sixteenth century to the day we live in, and which I have elsewhere attempted to explain, is in itself the indication of the remedy, *if* the study of art is to be healthily revived. As an evolutionary problem, it is one of the most interesting and not the least important in the history of culture. Is the question a purely historical one? Its practical solution is indicated more or less clearly by the analogies of every branch of the history of thought, and is shown with absolute precision in the philosophy of the arts taken collectively, their individual history, in which the law of evolution is shown, and, if we would study it, in the development of the individual artist; it is visible in music, in poetry, the dance, in sculpture, and in painting — sister arts where true arts, and as such subject to the same laws, and, in fact, only various forms of the same passion; that of expressing our emotions in rhythmic forms; of manifesting in communicable and sympathetic modes and ideal types the absolute and individual self. If the arts, born of one motive, appear in diverse guise, it is because each of our faculties demands a distinct appeal, and, for the satisfaction of its peculiar emotion, a distinct language. In each and all the artist is a creator, borrowing the language of nature only when it serves his purpose; but he is nowise her clerk or mirror —that is the mission of the scientist. But creation is governed by the law of evolution— nature did not escape this law and the artist cannot—the true art was evolved, the false art is borrowed.

Poetry and music have their motives and method so rooted in our spiritual natures that they can only be degraded by sensuality; but even then the art may keep its fineness, because, after all, the most intense sensuality has its roots in the spiritual nature, and it is only in its escape from the divine order and precedence that its vice lies. The dance we may consider a dependence of music; and these are immortal, in no peril of extinction. It is only to sculpture and painting that death can come; that form of death that keeps a body and loses the soul. Materialism is the deadly enemy of all the arts; but music and poetry cannot be materialised: they are born in human emotion, and will only die with it. Painting and sculpture are materialised by subjection to the facts of nature. They draw their language, the prime elements of their creation, from a visible world, so full in its vocabulary that the artist cannot escape from the suggestion of its terms, if he would be understood. Colour is, and in its highest expressions can only be, subjective, to be treated like music, orchestrally; but the element of form is necessarily dependent on nature for the intelligibility of its terms and types, the artist having only the faculty of exalting and refining her forms into what we recognise as the ideal; but the essential condition of all the arts of design becoming true art is in their being expression not imitation; that their statements and imagery shall be evolved from the mind of the artist, not copied from natural models; be creation, not repetition; and in the degree that this condition is fulfilled does the work become more or less purely a work of art. The form of materialism which menaces the arts of design is therefore science. The antagonism is inexorable but logical, and the position cannot be escaped from. Photography is the absolute negation of art; and if to-morrow it could succeed in reproducing all the tints of nature, it would only be the more antagonistic, if that were possible, to the true artistic qualities. "The letter killeth, the spirit giveth life," and though artistic creation does not involve the creation of the prime material, no more does, so far as science teaches, the creation of the world; the old material takes new forms, that is all. The idealist gets his materials from nature, but he recasts them in expression; the realist, who is no artist, repeats them as he gets them. This is the fundamental distinction in all design; the copyist is not an artist.

It is this and not the choice of subject, or the more or less decided tendency of a painter or a school, which constitutes the distinction between "high," or true art and "low," or spurious art; the test is not in fidelity to nature, but to one's own self. Giotto and Turner, Orcagna and Blake, Phidias and Michael Angelo, are alike types of the highest attainment; the modern realistic (? naturalistic) painters and the "Derby Day" school, the incident and costume painters of whatever school, are at the other end of the scale, more or less redeemed by purely technical power, but by no measure of it to be raised to the higher rank. Not that the distinction can be drawn sharply, so that we can in every case say that painters shall fall in one or the other category; but just in the proportion that an artist depends on his model or the actual material furnished by nature, so is he removed from pure art. Nature is a noble mistress, and there is nothing degrading in the most absolute subjection to her; but let us not for that confound the distinctions, the recognition of which lies at the bottom of sound criticism. The painter, whose devotion to nature is such that he never leaves or varies from her, may be, and is likely to be, a happier man than if he were a true artist; but he is not an artist any more than a photographer is one. Michael Angelo studied the human figure profoundly, probably more intensely than any modern painter, and worked from the knowledge he had acquired; but it is on record, and is shown by the internal evidence of his work, that he never worked directly from the model in his matured works. Giotto very certainly never used the model at all; and Turner never could paint from nature. To men of this type the external image disturbs the ideal, which is so complete that it admits no interference; as Turner is reported to have said, "Nature put him out," and this is a true condition. In Blake it was so developed that it became a morbid vision.

I have asked, without attempting to answer the question, in a prior essay, Is it necessary that art should be revived to the degree of importance it possessed in former times? I think not, but I hold my opinion as disputable. If the contrary is the truth, we must understand the law of the evolution of art and the element of our nature from which it draws its vitality, and not waste energy and existence in trying to make figs grow on thistles, or art at South Kensington. Some one said long ago what is to the profound student of religions a fundamental truth—"The nearer the church, the farther from God"; and in strict analogy with this I may say, the nearer to nature, the farther from art. I maintain it by the history of art, and by the demonstration of the law which governs all the arts of the ideals, as well as by the analysis of the method of working of the individual artist. This does not hinder that the church may become the guide to divine wisdom, as nature may lead to art, but never through slavery; but, to state it broadly, the subjection of reason to authority, or individual feeling to the hard and fast aspects of the physical world, is utterly antagonistic to the individuality which is the end of the development of the man or the artist. As religion was made for man, and not man for religion, so art was not made for nature, but nature for art, looking at the matter from the artist's point of view. The modern conception of the arts of design is that they are intended as the mirror of nature; the ancient and true one, that it was the outcome of the emotions, aspirations, and imaginative or spiritual conceptions of the artist; to the old master the facts of nature were the vocabulary of his language, to the new they are the types of his achievement; the former employed her forms to define his visions, the latter only mimics them; the former expresses an idea, the latter imitates a surface. Art has changed its public, forgotten its origin, and is no longer the teacher of humanity, the message of the gods, but the sycophant of vulgarity and ignorance; or, at its best —and would it were never worse employed!—the servant of science.

Who accepts nature as the supreme authority,

from which no appeal can lie, may be a scientist but never an artist. To the latter she offers suggestions but lays down no law. When what she brings him suits his purposes, he builds it in; when not, which is oftener the case, he hammers it into his own shape. Her facts are accidents; and what he wants is the very truth, the ideal.* If, from the beginning, his visions do not surpass the actualities he sees about him, if the passion of expression has not laid hold of him before the love of nature awakens in him, there is little or no probability of his having in him the material of success. The evolution of the individual follows the general law; and that, in all art, is that invention precedes imitation. Pure decoration with arbitrary forms, generally geometrical, precedes the representation of natural objects. This passion for decoration and the harmonious arrangement of forms, sounds, colours, or movements, is the essential element of all art. The love of nature is a distinct and completely subordinate element. Without the recognition of this law the development of a true and progressive art, the foundation of a school, is impossible. In music, the absolute subjection of the objective to the subjective, to the complete concealment of the former where it existed, makes the law clear to the dullest mind; in poetry, it is equally clear to those who have the ear for form, even if sometimes confused by those who confound the dignity

* The ideal of art is the perfection of form, but in nature all forms are accidental and imperfect.

of thought for the perfection of form, or, as in Whitman, mistaking the material for the form and ignoring the essential distinction between prose and poetry; but in painting and sculpture, the modern doctrine, ruinously, as earnestly and eloquently, maintained by Ruskin, gives the objective the absolute supremacy, making fidelity to nature the standard of excellence in art, completely reversing the artistic law. Until this heresy is recognised for what it is—pure fallacy—the arts of design can never be cultivated on the true basis.

What, then, is to be done to bring about a healthy revival of art on a foundation of education which shall secure its continued vitality? I am supposing, for the sake of my argument, that this is possible and necessary, of which I am not at all convinced. The first thing to be done, in the contrary case, is to banish from our criticism the false standard, and admit the possibility of a work of art being the better the less it is like nature (I do not say that divergence from nature is necessarily an approach to art, but that it may be so; in any case, the fidelity to nature has no relation whatever to the quality of the art); and to establish as the very foundation of the system of education that only the impression of nature is to be aimed at, even if it is in contradiction to the facts, and that memory and the record of impression are to be put in the first place in the acquisitions of the artist. We cannot go back to the childlike simplicity of all archaic art, with its dominant unsophisticated rendering of the central idea, and its normal and evolutionary attainment of perfection; we know too much of the fruit of the tree of knowledge to accept its greenness, and science has already too much forereached on art for the latter to begin again, with the capital of the days of Greek myths and the Italian reawakening, as all archaic art did, surrounded by the circumstances which excite the creative impulse, with the simplest, most direct expression of a dominant idea, and without reference to any non-essential facts, time and ripening knowledge adding step by step the deficient traits. What is to be done must be done with the recognition that we have been on a false road, on which we cannot now return, but must find the best cross-path to regain it. The simple satisfaction with which the artist in the childhood of art, as the child in his art, saw grow under his eye the image of his thought, is replaced by a mixed emotion in which the knowledge of the non-essential is too large a part to be slighted in the record.

And in this process we must return to the springs of art. The law is the same for all: the young poet trains his rhythmical sense by the reading of the best verse; the young musician in the music of his predecessors. The artist of form cannot escape from the law; if the emotion which inspires him is not supreme over all fact, remoulding, even suppressing or reversing it at need, casting it fused into the mould of his conception, if he does not accept the evolutionary

THE REVIVAL OF ART

law and absorb what went before him, his work will not be art. The distinction is radical and decides the very life of work or worker; it makes the difference between science and art, poetry and prose, music and talk, dance and locomotion; and the system of education which does not recognise and work from the distinction is doomed to eternal futility. From this there is no escape.

I appeal to the history of art. The earliest work of the great Greek school is scarcely distinguishable from the archaic work of all barbaric tribes; rude attempts to make visible an ideal, mostly of its conceptions of Deity, in which it is impossible not to see the analogy with the first efforts of children to shape resemblance of the things they love; this was, and is, invariably the presentation of conceptions, not studies from an object. The ideal was slowly worked out by the universal process of evolution, generation after generation working out the same problem of the ideal, the pupil carrying the work of his master a little further as he perceived the incompleteness of what was done before, but always in the sense of more perfect expression; finally arriving at a perception of nature idealised, the perfect types of beauty which no later epoch has re-discovered. And to the thorough student of Greek art it is brought home by a thousand details of internal evidence, that this slow attainment of perfection was the result, not of any system of copying nature, but by the gradual evolution, through centuries, of the perception of the ideal of form, attained through the simultaneous development of technical refinement and the power of retaining passing impressions of nature, and through the mutual reaction of these on each other.

The caviller will say that it matters not how the facts of nature came into the work—it was the nature, after all, which furnished the forms, and that the most perfect of the Greek works are those which are most like nature. But this is not true in fact, and is utterly false as generalisation. Nature never furnishes a perfect form, and supplies us with no criterion by which we can distinguish the more from the less beautiful. Nature tends to perfect beauty when she is regarded as a whole; but some of the noblest Greek statues contain violations of anatomical truth which no modern French sculptor would, or dare, be guilty of, but which were intentional and necessary to the beauty of form and expression. The artist found the lines and forms he wanted: where the anatomy came right it was because his memory was precise and tenacious, and the facts did not interfere with his ideal form; he saw the god in his imagination and gave him the form of highest beauty as he conceived it, and when in later days he saw the athlete in action, his memory retained the forms that gave the figure its expression; he knew nothing of anatomy or the function of the muscles, which, in the science of his day, were only the cushions which protected the bones in which all strength

THE REVIVAL OF ART

was supposed to lie; his vision of what was on the surface was undimmed by theories of what was underneath, and his powers of observation of every variation and characteristic of external form, and his retention of what he saw, were so highly developed that the use of the model was superfluous—his vision of the ideal was truer than the actuality of flesh and blood. This might seem incredible did we not know that it was the case with Michael Angelo, who worked on the marble without even a clay model to guide him.

Taking the entire course of Greek art from the most archaic period down to the Pergamenean school, we see that the development of the perfection of form was so slow as to be only recognised as an evolution, and no internal evidence of the direct copying of nature is to be found in the whole field; but when the intentional fidelity to nature becomes evident, as in the *Dying Gladiator* (although the *pose plastique*, which is the shadow of coming death to all art, is not yet apparent), we recognise that art is in its decline, fidelity to facts has begun to shoulder the perception of beauty, and the reign of the ideal has come to its end.

The same phenomenon appears in the history of the Italian Renaissance. The decay following the decline of all motives of art, in Greece, Rome, and Byzantium, consequent, perhaps, on the moral and political debasement, had brought all the arts to one dead level of mechanical achievement. Byzantine art is the synonym of all that is most mechanical and prescriptive, but with the possessions of its technique much was prepared for a revival, and the decorative instinct was always there potent and healthy. And out of the sleep of centuries came the new birth, not, as the fables run, from the inspiration of a single man or from a recognition of nature, but from the general awakening of the intellectual and moral life of Italy. Cimabue was only one of its manifestations. Sienna, if we had her record, might come before Florence, and certainly, in her Duccio, was superior to the master of Giotto —I am even inclined to believe not inferior to Giotto himself. But in Giotto we have the sum of all the qualities which told in the revival. What we find in his art is what we find in the early Greek, with something beyond, due to the evolution of humanity at large to a fuller life and a wider range of faculties; but it is an art of the ideal, not of the model; pure expression, in which the faculty of imaginative vision appears in a startling power, and in which there is the clearest internal evidence that he never used the model. His ideal differed from that of the Greek as the mediæval Italian did from the fellow-citizen of Pericles, and the ideal of the Renaissance was not that of physical perfection, but of spiritual glory and struggle, not of Apollo but of Christ. The intellectual processes are, however, the same. If, in the work of Giotto, the internal evidence of the purely ideal method be obscured, it is abundant in that of his pupils and immediate successors, whose absolutely subjective method is beyond dispute. And from Giotto onward there is a steady development in the direction of a larger comprehension of the qualities of the art and a fuller grasp of its alphabet; though, while in Giotto every detail is a part of his story and in his successors they become more or less conventional symbols, the underlying idea is the same. The undivided purpose of the work was the expression of the idea which inspired the artist, never the representation of nature except as a part of the vocabulary.

The climax of this ecstatic art came in Fra Angelico, not a great imagination but a wonderful visionary, whose pictures are probably the most perfect expressions we have of the purely subjective art, produced under the exaltation of religious emotion, and probably drawn from what the artist believed to be revelations of the heavenly world, and actually seen by him. The work of William Blake was probably as purely subjective, but there seems to me a taint of insanity in the vision; not the pure ecstacy kept, in Fra Angelico, a consistent element by the intensity of his religious passion, and in Blake replaced by an abnormal obsession. In the work of Fra Angelico's great pupil, Benozzo Gozzoli, I find for the first time the evidence of the direct and prosaic reference to nature for certain facts, forms, and the real semblance of the personages with whom the artist came in contact, and who became to a large extent the *dramatis personæ* of his pictures; but Gozzoli only made drawings from the person, which he used as memoranda when working on the picture. After him the practice became general to draw from the figure, and in some cases from cast draperies; but it is only in Fra Fillippo that we find the employment of actual types of the everyday world for the sacred personages, and not till long after that do we find the posing of the figure for dramatic action, while actual painting from life in the final work is not indicated till we reach the Carracci, in their so-called revival of art, which was really the death-blow to it. It is probable that Raphael and Titian drew their portraits from life on the canvas direct in the preparation, on which they afterward got their colour without the model; and, in the case of Titian, we have not only the internal evidence, but that of tradition to show that he did not paint from nature in the modern way, but on the basis of an accurate likeness, done in monochrome, followed by his conventional scheme of colour in the conventional technical method, borrowed from Bellini, and continued through the Venetian school till its close. All through the great period of the Renaissance the figures were evidently drawn from knowledge, in many cases acquired by the most severe drawing from nature, but the design was made from that knowledge, not from the model, which served merely for the better understanding of the subject. What the Greeks did we do not know by direct tradition, but we know that the absurd legends of their composing figures from the various members of different individuals, a leg from one and an arm from another, can have had no foundation in fact. No one who knows the *modus operandi* of the artistic mind can be in doubt as to that—no ideal image, even of a landscape, can be constructed in that way. The true idealist is he who, having the most complete knowledge of nature, uses her materials freely for his own purposes. She has her laws, and the idealist learns them and follows them as far as they serve his purposes.

The mental operations of the copyist and those of the idealist are diametrically opposed, whether the former copies nature or the work of another artist. With the former there is a constant measuring, comparing, a process of balancing in the mind far more laborious than the process of expression of conception in the imagination or memory. A modern school of painting has assumed the title of "impressionist," apparently ignorant of the fact that all true art is impressionist in the proper sense of the term, as all naturalistic representation is science, and not, strictly speaking, art at all. The majority of people nowadays prefer the latter: they know, more or less, what resembles what they see, and what they like; this world, familiar to them, may be worthier than that of the idealist and artist; that is a matter of taste not of discussion. But let us not confound terms and definitions—

if what we want is art, let us understand its character: if what we want is nature, let us recognise the fact and have done with it, but not wander in uncertainty as to what we are talking about.

Much of the confusion in the world of general thought on the subject of the ideal, is due to the confusion between the two accepted meanings of the word. The broad and comprehensive, and, therefore, the primary meaning, is the designation of what is present to the imagination as opposed to the palpable and materialised—the theory of the thing, as opposed to the accomplishment of it; the secondary meaning is something which is produced in conformity to that hypothetical perfection, because, as we recognise the imperfection of actual things, we admit that we must seek a perfect image in the regions of imagination—*i.e.*, of ideas. But, when we come to scientific discussion of the nature of art, we must recur to the primary use of the term, and recognise that whatever is the embodiment of a mental conception is ideal; and in any possible combination of the ideal and the actual, that part of the combination which makes it art is that which it owes to the mind of the artist, and not that which it derives from the material world. When, then, we propose to cultivate art by setting the would-be artist to painting from nature directly, we take a road which may in time permit him to become an artist, but which is not the true and direct way, and which may, indeed, divert him entirely from his aim, and is not, therefore, to be advised as the basis of an education, though it may be that best adapted to an education in what I will designate as scientific graphics, and the only method for men who have no ideal faculties. The essential conditions of a true art education, if we are to develop a genuine school, are the cultivation, above all others, of the faculties of rapid observation and retention of the significant facts, and putting before the eye the essential truths of what was seen, memorising the flitting panorama of nature and training the power of conception and the imagination by exercising and depending on them. Hamerton has given some most interesting observations on the method of memorising as a system of art training, and the history of modern art is full of cases of the power to be so attained. To work from knowledge of the reality of things, rather than from information of their superficial aspects, is the end to be kept in view: to get rid of the model as far as possible is the first step to the right education, dependence on the model the obstacle to it. The shadow of science is the eclipse of art.

I have said that I do not know that the revival of art is of any importance to humanity. I admit the possibility of its utter inutility to the spiritual or intellectual evolution of the race, of its having finished its work as an agent in that evolution, and having, in general, a purely historical value. I perceive, in the study of its history, that there have been epochs in which it served only to gratify vanity and ostentation, and it seems to me that we are now in such an epoch; but as in the past these morbid conditions have had reactions of healthy life, it is not permitted from an historical parallel to conclude that the future does not contain an art as genuine as any in the past. But two things must be noted by the philosophical student—viz., that the great evolutions of true art have always had their origin in some general passion supervening on the love of decoration, no fiat of ruler or official forcing-process ever having succeeded in initiating one; and that they have invariably been followed, and been stifled by, naturalistic tendencies. Nature has in every case killed art. The devotion to naturalism has, in all the past schools, been recognised by thoughtful criticism as the "decline of art." The reason is evident. The servile study of nature supersedes the exercise of those faculties on which I have shown the successful pursuit of art to depend; the vulgar taste applauds what it can understand—the superficial aspect of things, imitation, illusion, etc.; and the Academies, Royal and National, and the various societies, in their exhibitions and search of popularity, follow and confirm the vulgar opinion, which can never be otherwise than grossly ignorant; and only the artistic genius of inflexible fibre resists the current, and is generally ignored. The annual exhibitions are the grave of all that is best in art: individuality of the

THE REVIVAL OF ART

finer kind, refinement, simplicity which is a form of religion, and pure intellectual purpose — these are trampled out by the eager feet of those who give a morning to the work of a year, are unrecognised in the competition of brilliant technical surfaces, and are finally buried in the ignorant comment of the hurried daily press, compelled to pronounce judgment without consideration, and generally without the most elementary knowledge of the subject. No labour of any human worker is ever subjected to such degradation as is art to-day under the criticism of the daily paper. Now and then a true artist fights his way to his proper place by sheer intellectual power and patient endurance; but others, as true in aim, if of minor force, are never recognised till they are dead, if even then.

Under the hypothesis, then, that art is to be revived and cultivated, the study of the works and methods of the genuine schools of art in past times is of the highest and primary importance—is, in fact, the foundation of our schools to be. The mimicry of ancient forms, the adoption of antique or mediæval themes, or the affectation of a manner that was spontaneous to a mind that came to activity under influences utterly diverse from those under which we live, have nothing to do with art, and in no wise aid us. Whether the Greeks believed in the gods whose images they carved, or the Cinquecentists in the holy men and women they painted, is to us utterly immaterial. What they have given us is the method by which they attained excellence in art, and the law at the root of it. That their faith in their saints had anything to do with that excellence I do not believe, or that any revival of such faith is necessary for a new art. The history of art does not indicate it, and the biography of the artists denies it. What the old art teaches, in whatever form it took, is that the art is in the artist, and not in nature; and from Archermos to Praxiteles, as from Cimabue to Raphael, the development is one of accumulating knowledge going hand-in-hand with an increasing skill and technical resources, in which the evidence is unmistakable to who can read it, that the study of nature was indirect, and that scientific knowledge of things never came to disturb the order of ideal creation. The Greek sculpture was not cursed by a knowledge of anatomy; and, after Michael Angelo had introduced it, the sculpture of Italy became a mere muscular inanity. We cannot now go so far as to ignore anatomy, but we can cease to study it, and recognise no more of it than the Greek could see and show; no more of it than is necessary to express the idea that animates us, remembering always that fidelity to the conception is the first obligation of art, fidelity to nature a secondary matter, and sometimes counter-indicated by the primary law, and out of the question.

These considerations only add, however, to the gravity of the question I have already asked and which no individual can answer, but a race and

THE REVIVAL OF ART

an epoch—Does the world want art any longer? Has it, in the present state of human progress, any place which will justify the devotion to it of the class of minds which once found in it the enthusiasm of their youth and the content of their ripe years? Is it with the race, as with the individual, that—

> "There was a time when meadow, grove, and stream,
> The earth, and every common sight,
>   To me did seem
> Apparelled in celestial light,
> The glory and the freshness of a dream.
> It is not as it has been of yore;
>   Turn whereso'er I may,
>   By night or day,
> The things which I have seen I now can see no more"?

and must we be content, like the apostle of nature, the passion and exaltation of the youth of humanity being outgrown, to look back at what the bloom-time has left us, and—

> ". . . . rather find
> Strength in what remains behind,
> In the primal sympathy
> Which having been must ever be:
> In the soothing thoughts that spring
> Out of human suffering;
> In the faith that looks through death,
> In years that bring the philosophic mind"?

Is not this unquestionable indication of the operation of the law of collective evolution on the progress of the race an indication also of the futility of our schemes for collective art education? Is it not the case that the feeling which alone can make fruitful all these schemes now only occurs in rare individuals who may be considered survivals of a prior and more youthful state of humanity, which is now in the "years that bring the philosophic mind"? No one can admit that the human intellect is weaker than it was five or twenty centuries ago; but it is certain that if we take the pains to study what was done five centuries ago in painting, or twenty centuries ago in sculpture, and compare it with the best work of to-day, we shall find the latter trivial and 'prentice work compared with the ordinary work of men whose names are lost in the lustre of a school.

Then, little men inspired by the Zeitgeist, painted greatly; now, our great men fail to reach the technical achievement of the little men of them. There is only one living painter who can treat a portrait as a Venetian painter of 1550 A.D. would have done it, and how differently in the mastery of his material! If we go to the work of wider range, the Campo Santo of Pisa, the Stanze, the Sistine Chapel, the distance becomes an abyss; the simplest fragment of a Greek statue of 450 B.C. shows us that the best sculpture of this century, even the French, is only a happy child-work, not even to be put in sight of Donatello or Michael Angelo. The reason is simple, and already indicated. The early men grew up in a system in which the power of expression was taught from childhood; they acquired method as the musician does now, and the tendency of the opinion of their time was to keep them in the good method.

Beginning as apprentices, they grew to be masters; art was not a diversion, but a serious occupation, to which fathers sent their sons when boys as to other trades, and they learned to express ideas as soon as ideas began to form, and before they had acquired scientific perception; and, having acquired the power to express thought, power grew as the thought enlarged. We begin late as amateurs; we see surfaces, and contemporary taste likes surfaces, but nothing serious; we lean on the model, and cannot escape it because we dare not risk to be caught out of drawing; the conception is never clear because we never trust it, and we must compare our work, touch by touch, with the model; we are never free, and we end in *pose plastique*, the caricature of art. The purely mechanical habit of reproducing the thing set before us, deferring to scientific exactitude as if it were authority in art, has little by little extinguished in the modern mind the sense of the ideal, just as an absorption in the material life in its insatiable and ever-increasing claims, stifles, and finally entirely eliminates, the spiritual faculties. If there be no vital relation between the two, there is, at least, an analogy. I shall not discuss the question whether religion — by which I mean the spiritual life, not a creed or a church — is necessary to human progress or happiness, any more than I should maintain that art, in its highest acceptation, is so; indeed, I have honest doubts whether art is necessary or greatly useful; but I have the clearest perception of the truth that, in the one case as in the other, the devotion to the material stifles the ideal. The natural sciences, the model, Fact—which is accident, fidelity to nature, to use the common term —is the negation of the ideal and the extinction of the perception of the beautiful, which are in turn the highest witnesses of the spiritual life. Few men love nature more than I do, and few have spent time in more patient and reverential record of her material features by the most scrupulous·copying of landscape; but I recognise that if I had ever possessed the higher gifts of the artist, this devotion to the shell of nature was the most efficient method for their extinction.

I know nothing more melancholy to one who has gone through the university of art, the silent schools of the long-past centuries—Greece, Tuscany, Venice, Holland of the Van Eycks, and Germany of Dürer—than to walk through a modern art exhibition and hear the comments of a public which, if not wise, is the only one art has to look to; the enthusiasm for the superficialities and unintelligent reproduction of a world of accidents, spending its admiration on tricks of the brush and curiosities of texture, while the genuine expressions of artistic feeling, *rari nantes in gurgite vasto*, soon to be forgotten as well, are passed with a joke or a sneer of incomprehension as affectations or absurd archaisms; or, what is almost as fatal in education in art, respected not because they are the result of the real art motive, but on account of some incidental characteristic of the artist, an eccentricity which is attributed to a peculiarity of vision, or the discovery of a new process of painting. But this is the condition of public appreciation, not only in England and America, but even in France, where the national temperament is more favourable to the development of æsthetic feeling.

As I have said, no individual can answer the question I have asked—Do we want art any longer? But if I were called on to answer my own question, I would say, No! We want portraiture, because the leading motive in the majority is vanity, and the highest virtue domestic affection. For the awakening of the highest artistic faculties we have neither the desire nor the ability. We understand vaguely what is like nature, and we confound the representation of nature with art. People who take to art in the feeling that it is a better amusement than any other, are too far advanced in life to acquire a really noble execution, just as they would be in music; and they always depend on nature because it is the easiest way to get along. The establishment of schools in the old and true sense of the word, where the training should begin with the development of the intellect, and correct habits of working should be acquired before the critical faculties are at work, in which a regular apprenticeship should be gone through, the process by which alone a master can be made, is, in the present state of things, impossible. If in some more or less remote future a reaction should follow the present temper and art find a new world, we may have prepared the way for it by the recognition of its true principles, and, above all, the clear understanding that its fundamental law is that in its sphere art is supreme, and nature only its bricks and mortar. So long as we confound fidelity to nature with excellence in art, we ignore that law.

NOTE.—The following quotations from a note of Mr Watts, which I am permitted to make public, written after reading the foregoing essay in MS., will certainly entitle the views which they discuss to a certain degree of consideration, and will have an intrinsic value as the conclusions of one whom I am compelled to regard as the profoundest thinker on art with whose opinions I am conversant:—

"I agree so much with the general tenor of your article that it is what I am always saying. There are two or three points I might wish to discuss upon the question of art education. Certainly I do not think modern art education a good one, but I think education in art necessary. The language of art is not quite a natural one, since it is not possessed by all. The great artist, like the great poet, may forget his means as he forgets himself in his work; but to do this, his means must be entirely sufficient. When Wordsworth wrote the "Imitations of Immortality," he never had to think of his grammar or his spelling: such a necessity must have crippled his utterances. The soldier fighting for his life does not think about the rules of fence, but for the perfect handling of his weapons, and he has had to learn to use them. The greatest art must deal with the human figure, the strongest appeal to humanity can only be made through humanity. Michael Angelo was not a better artist for giving twelve years to the study of anatomy, perhaps the worse; but a very considerable knowledge of, and acquaintance with, the structure of the human frame is absolutely necessary, an acquaintance difficult for him to acquire in northern climates and in modern times. The artist acquainted with the human structure through the medium of his restricted observation alone, will find himself in the position of the musician who composes by ear. This may suffice for his melody, but without knowledge of counterpoint he will not be able to set down in writing the complications of his harmony. Painting from the model is a thing I entirely disapprove of: I never do it and have never done it, never setting up the model in a fixed position, though referring to it occasionally when knowledge or memory may be at fault; but there should be no hesitation for want of knowledge, and the more elevated the intention the more necessary that there should be no obvious violations of grammar in art. Also, I think that you should make it understood that you admit that even painting from still life and subjects where dexterous imitation and beautiful workmanship are interesting and pleasing, is still art in a degree and worthy of praise, as all things done conscientiously are: this, while you rightly insist that reality is fatal to the dignity of higher endeavour. . . . I should not like my method of study to be misunderstood: though not painting from the model, I do not depend upon knowledge, still less memory, alone, but, for example, get any one who may be about to lend me a wrist or an elbow, not merely in the position required but turning the joint about, not to copy but to refresh my knowledge. This is probably what Phidias did with greater opportunities. I do the same thing—that is to say, study more than I have immediate occasion to represent when painting a portrait. For example, if I am painting a full-face, I endeavour to learn the profile, that I may not depend on the light and shadow alone for the form of the features. I do not hesitate to repeat that I consider the painting from the model in a set position a pernicious practice, but the study of nature is another thing and cannot be dispensed with. . . . I think you may have remarked that I purposely avoid display of anatomical knowledge in my figures, and all reference to creeds in my subjects."

These views of the great artist are in no wise in conflict with those I have tried to expound, though, as he writes in the nature of a general approval, he dwells on the points on which he desires to qualify my statements; but I do not exclude a lower form of art, which I have noted as "low, or spurious art," and the excellence of which is in the perfection of its means, not in the nobility of its ends, and to be respected as we should respect a versifier whose grammar and diction were faultless, but who was quite devoid of poetic inspiration. Nature is noble, and the most scrupulous rendering of her, in every attainable aspect, is worthy commendation as handicraft; but even here we are in a way which leads to the antipodes of the true and supreme art—that of the ideal, the creative. There is one honour of the hand and another of the brain, and they rarely go to the same work.

THE SUBJECTIVE OF IT

TOWARDS the close of a dreamy August day, in company with a half-dozen friends, members of that circle of literary men who made the American Cambridge more eminent in American literary life than it has been before or since, I was watching the waning of the day in our camp on the sheet of water in the Adirondacks known as "Tupper's Lake," and mingling in a desultory conversation, ranging from rifles and the shape of the bullets we used, to spiritualism. The camp was built on the bold shore of the lake, whose waters, the untremulous mirror of the mountains and unbroken forest around and the cloudless sky above, showed only in blue fragments through the interstices of the leafy veil that shut us in. The forest was unbroken to the water's edge, and even out over the water itself the firs and cedars stretched their gaunt limbs, with here and there a moisture-loving white birch, so that from the very shore one sees only suggestive bits of sky and distance; while from where we were lying, sky, hills, and water were all blue alike, and undistinguishable alike, glimpses of a world of sunshine which the cool and grateful shadow we lay in made more delicious to the thought. We were sheltered in right woodsman's style; our little house of fresh-peeled bark of spruces, twelve feet by nine, open only to the east, towards the lake, protected us from wind and rain, and the primeval forest shut round us so closely that no eyes could pierce a pistol shot into their green recesses. There were blue-jays about us, making the woods ring with their querulous cries, and a single osprey could be heard circling and screaming above the water as he sailed, watching for a supper in the lake.

Three of the party were asleep; the others, amongst whom was Lowell, talked desultorily, quietly and low, as if the drowsiness had half conquered them too. The conversation had turned to spiritualism, through my narrating some singular experiences I had met with in the way of presentiments and second-sight during a three months' sojourn in the woods the summer before. There is something wonderfully exciting to the imagination in the wilderness, after the first impression of monotony and lonesomeness has gone, and there comes the necessity to animate this so vacant world with something; to people it if even with shadows. And so the pines lift themselves grimly against the twilight sky, and the moanings of the woods become full of meaning and mystery. Living, therefore, as I had done in the wilderness, summer after summer, until there is no place in the world so much like a home to me as a bark "camp" in the Adirondack, I had come to be what most people would call morbid, but what I felt to be simply sensitive to the things around, which we never see, but to which we at times pay the deference of a tremor of inexplicable fear, a quicker and less deeply-drawn breath, an involuntary turning of the head to see something which we know we shall not see and are glad that we do not, all which things we laugh at as childish when they have passed, yet tremble at as readily when they come again.

Lowell, in spite of the poet in him, had a strong vein of metaphysic, and looked at those matters with a cold analysis; and yet his imagination at times was so active that his images worked out their own solutions, while he looked on, and he had wonders to tell of, passing mine by a degree; his experiences were more remarkable than mine, and yet he had an explanation for everything which I could not put aside, though not always convinced. "Yes," said he, as he rose and knocked the ashes out of his meerschaum to join in the row the doctor suggested to watch the sunset from the lake, "yes, I believe in your kind of spiritual world, but that it is purely subjective." I was silenced in a moment. This single sentence, spoken like the conviction of a lifetime, produced an effect his logic had not. He had opened to me a new world of marvels and mysteries; he had not convinced me that I was wrong in my own theories, so much as opened to suggestion new paths of explanation, and had turned the spiritual world into myself. The phase of spiritual existence which had been real to me melted away into the thinness of an incompleted dream; but as it melted, it revealed a real world beyond, which I had not dreamed of before, or at least had never realised in the true sense of the term. Still, amongst phantoms, the subjective world flamed out on me as the world beyond all things. I had played with the words and phrases relating to Subjectivity and Objectivity, and understood them as terms of logic, but now their reality suddenly flashed on me, seen in the round. I looked through the range of human cognitions, and found from beginning to end only the proclamation of the presence of the arch-magician, Imagination. I had often said to myself: "The universe is subjective to Deity, objective to me; but if I am in His image, what is that in me which corresponds to the Creator in Him?" Here I found myself at last, the creator of a universe of unsubstantialities all of the stuff that dreams are made of, and all alike unconsciously evoked, whether the dreams of sleep or the hauntings of waking hours. I grew bewildered as the realisation of the thought, not merely its intellectual perception, loomed up in its infinite significance; and a thousand facts and phenomena, which had been standing around my little circle of vision, burst into light and recognition, as though they had been waiting beyond the verge for the magic words. Lowell had spoken them.

Silent, almost for the moment unconscious of external things, I walked down to the shore. Taking our seats in one of the boats, we pushed off on the quiet water. There was no flaw in the mirror which gave us a duplicated world.

Line for line, tint for tint, the noble mountain that lifted itself at the east, robed in primeval forest to its very summit, and then suffused with the rosy light of the setting sun, sunk behind the ridge behind us, was reproduced in the void below. The shadows of the western upland began to climb the opposite bluffs of the lake shore. We pulled well out into the lake and lay on our oars. If anything was said I do not remember it. I was as one who had just heard words from the dead, and hears as prattle all the sounds of common life. My eyes, my ears, were opened anew to nature, and it seemed as if a new sense had been given me. I felt as I had never felt before, the cold gloom of the shadow creep up, ridge after ridge, towards the solitary peak, irresistibly and triumphantly encroaching on the light which fought back towards the summit, where it must yield at last. It drew back over ravines and gorges, over the unbroken wildernesses of firs which covered all the upper portion of the mountain, deepening its rose tint, and gaining in intensity what it lost in expanse, diminished to a hand-breadth, to a point, and, flickering an instant, went out, leaving in the whole range of vision no speck of sunlight to relieve the immensity of gloomy shadow. I had come under a spell; for, often as I had seen the sunset in these mountains and over the lakes, I had never before felt as I now felt—that I was a part of the landscape, and that it was to me something more than rocks and trees. The sunlight had died on it. Holmes took up the oars, and our silently-moving boat broke the glassy surface again. All around us no distinction was visible between the landscape above and that below, no water-line could be found; and to the west, where the sky was still glowing and golden, with faint bands of crimson cirrus flaming along across the deep and tremulous blue, growing violet as the sun sank lower, we could distinguish nothing in the landscape but vague and vacillating waves of retreating forest. Neither sound nor motion of animate or inanimate thing disturbed the scene, save that of the oars, with the long lines of blue which ran off from the wake of the boat into the mystery closing behind us. A rifle-shot rang out from the landing and rolled in multitudinous echoes around the lake, dying away in faintest thunders and murmurs from the ravines which harrowed the mountain-sides. It was the call to supper, and we pulled back to the light of the camp-fire which was now glimmering through the trees which shut in our camp.

Supper over, the smokers lighted their pipes, and a rambling conversation began on the sights and sounds of the day. For my part, unable to quiet the uneasy questioning which possessed me, or to take part in a conversation which had no meaning for me in my mood, I wandered down to the shore, and, entering my boat, pushed idly out into the lake to be alone. The uneasy question still stirred within me; and now, looking towards the north-west, where the sky still glowed faintly with the failing twilight, a long line of pines, gaunt and humanesque as no other tree but our North-American white pine is, was relieved in massy blackness against the golden grey, like a procession of giants. They were mostly in groups of two or three, with now and then an isolated one, stretching along the horizon, losing themselves in the gloom of the northern mountains. The weirdness of the scene caught my excited imagination in an instant, and I became conscious of two mental phenomena. The first was an impression of motion in the trees, as if they were marching eastward, which, whimsical as it was, I had not the power to dispel. I trembled from head to foot under the consciousness of this supernatural vitality. My rational faculties were as clear as ever they had been, and I understood perfectly that the semblance of motion, delusive as it was, was owing to two characteristics of the pine—viz., that it follows the shores of the lakes in long lines, rarely growing at a distance from the water, except when it follows, in the same orderly arrangement, the rocky ridges; and that, from its height above all the other forest trees, it catches the full force of the prevalent westerly winds, and grows, slightly leaning to the east, like a person walking. These traits of the trees explained entirely the phenomenon; yet the knowledge of them had not the least effect on my imagination, which remained deluded. I was awestruck, as though the phantoms of some antedeluvian race had risen from the Adirondack valleys, and were marching in silence to their old fanes on the mountain-tops. I cowered in the boat under an absolute nervous chill of apprehension.

The second phenomenon was that I heard a voice which said distinctly these words, "The procession of the Anakim!" and, at the same moment, I became conscious of some disembodied spiritual being standing near me, as we sometimes are aware of the presence of a friend without having seen him. Everybody accustomed to solitary thought has probably recognised this form of mental action, and speculated on the strange duality of our natures implied in it. The spiritualists call it "impressional communication," and abandon themselves to its vagaries in the belief that it is the speech of angels; thinking men find in it a mystery of our mental organisation, and avail themselves of it under the direction of their reason. I at present speculated with the philosophers; but my imagination, stronger than my reason, refused the explanation, and assured me that something spoke. I sat still as long as, alone, I could keep down the spectral horror that grew on me, and, paddling back to the landing, I took refuge in the camp, feeling only reassured in the presence of my companions.

But even then my attendant Dæmon did not leave me, for now I heard the question, asked in a taunting tone, "Subjective or objective?"

I asked myself in reply: "Am I sane or mad?"

"Quite sane, but with your eyes opened to

something new!" was the reply, as instantaneous as thought.

On such occasions as ours, men get back easily to the primitive usage and conditions of humanity. We had arisen at dawn; darkness brought the desire to rest. Our beds were made of the boughs of the fir-trees, spread over the flooring of the "shanty," with a trimming of the twigs of the fragrant *Arbor Vitæ*, on which we spread ourselves, side by side, with our feet to a huge camp-fire, and all except myself were soon asleep. I lay long, excited, watching the occasional gleam of a star through the boughs overhead, and finding in their twinkling further sign of my fellowship with nature, my new state of existence, and they seemed to be winking to me as to one who shared the secret of their existence. The moaning of the tall pine trees overhead had a new sound and significance, which it seemed as if I must come to understand — everything was new and strange — nature and I had everything in common. I slept at length -- a strange kind of sleep; for when the guides awoke me in broad daylight, I was conscious of a feeling as if someone had been talking with me all night.

In broad day, with my companions, and in motion, the terror passed, and the influences of the previous evening seemed to keep a distance; but I was aware that they were in waiting for the moment when I should be alone again. The day was as brilliant, as tranquil as its predecessor, and the council decided that it should be devoted to a deer drive, for we had eaten the last of our venison at breakfast. The members of the company were assigned their places at the points where the deer was most likely to pass to take the water, while, with my guide, Steve Martin, I went up Bog River to start him. The river—a dark, sluggish stream, about fifty feet wide—is the outlet of a chain of lakes above, and is a favourite feeding-ground for the deer who come for the leaves of the *Nuphar Lutea* which partly fill the stream. We surprised one, and giving him a shot as he went out, I wounded him, but not seriously enough to stop his running, and landing, we put the dog on his track and went back to wait. The deer ran back into the hills, and we could only follow his motions by the occasional baying of the hound. It came and went, circling round, and the old habit of the hunter came to fill my mind and chase away the pre-occupations of the night. The purely animal excitement of the chase is, perhaps, the best remedy for an over-strained mind, and I was for the moment a beast of prey. As the deer, after twice doubling, had taken the direction of the lake, we felt sure that he would take the water there, and we slowly paddled down stream. The emotions of the hunt had, as I thought, brought me back to a natural state of mind; and as I lay in the stern of the boat, looking up at the blue sky, steeping in the healthy sunlight which penetrated soul and body, and the brain lulled into lethargy by the unbroken silence and monotony of the scene, I looked back to the experience of the night before as a curious dream. I asked myself wherein it differed from a dream, and instantly my Dæmon replied, "In nowise." The instant reply startled me, but the sunshine had dispelled the terror, and I asked, as a matter of course, "But if no more than a dream, it amounts to nothing." It answered me, "But when a man dreams wide awake?" I pondered and hesitated in my thought, and it went on, "And how do you know that dreams are nothing? They are as real, while they last, as your waking thoughts; your dream-life imposes on your consciousness with the impression of its reality—your waking-life does no more; you wake to one and sleep to the other. Which is the real and which the false, since you assume that one is false?" I could only ask myself again the eternal question, "Objective or subjective?" and the Dæmon made no further suggestion. At this instant we heard the report of a gun from the lake, and Steve said, "The deer is in—that's the doctor's shot-gun." And we knew that the deer was killed, as the doctor had a double-barrelled shot-gun, and if he had missed with the first shot would have fired the second, and we pulled back to camp.

Arriving at the landing, we found the guides dressing the deer and the company preparing for dinner. The rest of the day passed in fishing, in exploring the nooks and islands of the lake, and my usual frame of mind returned. As the

THE SUBJECTIVE OF IT

night came on, the excitement of the evening before returned, and I determined to stay in camp through the evening; not that I feared the ghostly society which had haunted me out on the lake, for with the experience it had become familiar, but I wanted to see if the mental action was produced by solitude, or if it would come in society. The company went in part out for a row, and part sat down to cards by candle light and the huge fire of green logs. I retired to the shanty and threw myself down on my blankets; but then I felt the Dæmon sitting by me, ready to be questioned.

Then came suddenly a flash of doubt as to the theological status of my ghostly *vis-à-vis*, and I abruptly asked, "Who are you?" "Nobody," replied the Dæmon, oracularly.

This I knew in one sense to be true, and I replied, "But you know what I mean. Don't trifle. Of what nature is your personality?"

"Do you think," it replied, "that personality is necessary to existence? We are spirit."

"But wherein, save in the having or not having a body, do you differ from me?"

"In all the consequences of that difference."

"Very well, go on."

"Do you not see that without your circumstances you are only half a being? that you are shaped by the action and reaction between your own mind and surrounding things, and that your mind is only the medium of this action and reaction? Do you not see that without this there would have been no consciousness of self, and consequently neither individuality nor personality? Remove those circumstances by removing the body, and do you not remove personality?"

"But," said I, "you certainly have individuality, and wherein does that differ from personality?"

"Possibly you commit two mistakes," replied the Dæmon. "As to the distinction, it is one with a difference. You are personal to yourself, individual to others; and we, though individual to you, may still be impersonal. If spirit takes form from having something to act on, the fact that we act on you is sufficient, so far as you are concerned, to develop individuality."

I hesitated, puzzled.

It went on: "Don't you see that the inertia of spirit is motion, as that of matter is rest? Now, compare this universal spirit to a river flowing always but tranquilly, and which in itself gives no evidence of motion, save where it meets with some inert point of resistance. This point of resistance has the effect of action in itself, and you attribute to it all the eddies and ripples produced. You must see that your own immobility is the cause of the phenomena of life which give you your own apparent existence; our individuality to you may be just as much the effect of your own personality; you find us responsive only to your own mental state."

I was conscious of a sophistry somewhere, but could not for the life of me detect it. I thought of the Tempter; I almost feared to listen to another word; but the Dæmon seemed so fair, so rational, responding only to my questions, and above all so confident of truth, that I could not entertain my fears.

"But," said I finally, "if my personality is owing to my physical circumstances, to my body and its inertiæ, what is the body itself owing to?"

"All physical or organic existence is owing to the antagonism between particles of matter, fixed and resistant, and the all-pervading, ever-flowing spirit, the different inertiæ conflict; and end by combining in an organic being, since neither can be annihilated or transmuted. Perhaps we may tell you after a time how this antagonism commences; at present you would hardly be able to comprehend it clearly."

This I felt, for I was already getting confused with the questions that suggested themselves to me as to the relations between spirit and matter. I asked once more, "Have you never been personal, as I am, for instance? Have you not at some time had a body and a name?"

"Perhaps," was the reply; "but it was so long ago, and the trifling circumstances you call living, with all their direct and recognisable effects, pass away so soon, that it is impossible to recall anything of it. There seems a kind of consciousness when we have something to act against, as against your mind at the present moment; but as to name, and all unsubstantial distinctiveness, what is the use of them where there is no possibility of confusion or mistake as regards an identity which has not the most trivial importance? We have said that we are spirit; and when we say that matter is one and spirit one, we have gone behind individual identity."

"But," asked I, "am I to lose my individual existence, to become finally merged in a universal impersonality? What, then, is the object of life?"

"You see the plants and animals all around you growing up and passing away—each entering its little orbit, and sweeping through this sphere of cognisance back again to the same mystery that it emerged from; you never ask the question as to them, but for yourself you are anxious. If you had not been, would creation have been the less creation? If you cease, will it not still be as great? Truly, though, your mistake is one of too little, not of too much. You assume that the animals will be annihilated; but, in fact, nothing dies. The very crystals into which the so-called primitive substances are formed, and which are the first forms of organisation, have a spirit in them. If you could decompose the crystal, would you annihilate what made it such? The plant decomposes and absorbs the crystal, and it becomes a part of a higher, or more complex organisation, equally dependent on the originating motive; and, if it is cut down and cast into the oven, is the organic element food for the flames. You, the animal, do but exist through the absorption of these vegetable and derived substances, and why should you claim exemption from the analogical law of absorption and aggregation? You killed a deer to-day—the flesh you will appropriate to supply the wants of your own material organisation; but the life, the spirit which made that flesh a deer, in obedience to which that shell of external appearance is moulded—you missed that. You can trace the body in its metamorphoses; but for this impalpable, active, and only real part of the being, it were folly to assume that it is more perishable, more evanescent than the matter of which it was the master. And why should not you, as well as the deer, go back into the Great Life from which you came? As to the purpose in creation, why should there be any other than that which existence always shows, of creation?"

I was silent, pondering as to how I should form my questions on a subject which seemed to me that of Hamlet, to be or not to be, and the Dæmon, as if following my thought, said: "Do not understand that we affirm or the contrary as to what you consider the indispensable form of being—we only seek to put your own ideas on the subject on the true path; we cannot help you to more truth than you have fitted your mind to assimilate. You puzzle yourself uselessly on the finer distinctions which must be drawn to make the distinction between matter and spirit clear. Your ideas are stereotyped in certain forms, and that which does not find its type amongst those you know is not recognisable by you. Is there any distinction which you can recognise between you and the deer you killed to-day, which justifies you in assuming a right to immortality and future individuality that the deer had not? Are you who daily violate the laws of your spiritual existence more worthy than he who never violated one?"

I had been slowly coming to the perception of the fact that all the leading ideas of the Dæmon were put in the form of questions, as if from a cautious non-committalism, or as if it dared not in plain words affirm that they were the absolute truth. I felt that there was another side to the matter, and was confident that I should sooner or later detect the sophistry of my Dæmon; but then I did not feel competent to carry the subject further, and was sensible of a readiness on the part of my interlocutor to cease. I wondered at this, and if it implied weariness on its part, and it was instantly replied: "We always answer to your mind; when that ceases to act, there ceases to be the reaction." I cried out in my mind in utter bewilderment "Objective or subjective?" and, longing for some diverson of my mind from the train of thought, called on the guides to make a "blaze," and I felt that the physical light would be a relief to the mental obscurity. In the course of a few minutes, the guides had piled on the fire a huge mass of the finer branches of the trees which had served us for fuel, and the immense column of flames which rose, frightening the birds from their perches, into a confused clamour, threw into the shanty a heat which made me drowsy, and when my companions returned from their row I was asleep.

It was determined the next morning in council to move; and one of the guides informing me that there had been opened a new "carry" by which we might cross from the Upper Tupper's Lake, ten miles up the Bog River, directly to the Forked Lake, and thence following the usual route down the Raquette River and through Long Lake, we could reach Martin's on Saranack Lakes, where we should find our conveyances out to the settlements, with only a short retracing of the road we had come by, we hurriedly packed our traps after breakfast and were off.

The boating up Bog River is hard work; there are many shallows over which the boats must be dragged, and "carries" round which everything must be carried on the backs of the men, one of these being three miles long, so that, work as we all might, the day had drawn to a close before we were well embarked on the upper lake, and it was nightfall before we reached the camp, left by a former visitor, where we intended to sleep. I had worked hard all day, always sharing the work of the guides, but in a dreamy state, as if the dead-weights I carried were only the phantoms of something, and I was a fantasy carrying them —the actual had become visionary, and my imaginations nudged and jostled me almost off the ways of reason. But I had no time for a *séance* with the Dæmon, and the fatigue left me too disposed for sleep to allow of night-questionings.

The next day we had several miles of new paths to bush out, cutting the smaller trees, for we found the information as to the road to be incorrect; so that, in fact, we had two days of severe chopping and dragging before we were again in boating regions. All this had put me into a healthier state of mind than I had been in for a long time, for I had come into the woods very much exhausted by overwork, to which was due, probably, my wanderings of imagination; and the day or two following, devoted to the work of the camp, with the necessary fishing and hunting required to keep a large party of men with renewed appetites, gave me, the master of the hunt and commissary-general, too much to do to think of mental phenomena. But the hurry over and repose come, the mental condition returned. Recommencing the migration towards home, we ran down the lake to its outlet, and, as we turned a point, a wide and picturesque view came into sight—a long vista, at the extreme distance of which rose a faint, solitary peak, to which Steve pointed, saying with a tone of emphasis, "Blue Mountain." The effect was to attach to the distant peak the glamour of the mental condition in which I had been: a strange and unaccountable attraction to it came over me, as if some fatality awaited me there, the solution of the mysterious influences which I had been under during the days past. I have thought of it since, many times; and have noticed in more than one case of insanity with which I had come into contact, that when the diseased mind had been prepared by some circumstance for a new delusion, the slightest trifle sufficed to create it. From that moment my mind was "suggestioned," to use a word much employed lately to define what we still cannot any better explain, by the idea of something to be seen or learned at the Blue Mountain, of which the only notable fact that I could learn was that it was, as I could see, a solitary peak in the midst of a chain of small lakes, difficult of access, and, therefore, almost unvisited. My plans for the summer were to see my friends through their visit to the lakes; and when they had used up their vacation to see them off, and return to the most primeval forest remaining and spend the remainder of the summer there, until the cold of autumn drove me back. The run down the Raquette River occupied several days of motion and hard work, and there was no opening for my delusions. The company once consigned to civilisation again, I took my way back to the upper waters, and with Steve and Carlo alone for society, built myself a comfortable camp on the Raquette Lake, within sight of the Blue Mountain. Steve objected to fighting our way up there; for, after all, we were still more or less dependent on the half-civilisation of the trappers and squatters who were here and there to be found on the principal lakes, where they carried on in winter the business of "lumbering," cutting and hauling the trees which form the value of the mountain region, too remote from all communication with the ways of commerce to be useful for cultivation, and too barren when the forest is cleared away. The occasional log-cabins, which form the headquarters for the lumbermen in the winter, generally furnish supplies for the hunters and fishermen for the part of the year when sporting is possible, and from them we were obliged to draw our flour, salt pork, etc. etc., which, with the game and fish which we caught, formed our subsistence. On the Blue Lakes there was not a settler, and for many miles from it, measured as the distances are there measured, through labyrinths of forest and meandering streams, which are often the only way by which, with great labour, one can force his way through, no human habitation existed. Steve had not my motive for getting there, and knew the hardships too well to be willing to put himself in the way of them uselessly: his wood-craft was older than mine, and so I submitted to his judgment and we camped on Raquette Lake. In all the operations of settling for some weeks, finding subjects for my sketching and making the camp comfortable, my mind was healthily occupied, and I heard nothing of my ghostly friend; till, one evening when I had paddled out on the lake to enjoy the night and the multitude of its stars, which never elsewhere seemed so great as in that pure air, I felt it beside me without warning.

"Well," I said, "you have come back."

"Come back!" it said. "Will you never get rid of your miserable notions of space, and learn that there is no separation but that of feeling, no nearness but that of sympathy? If you had cared enough to be near us, we should have been with you constantly."

I was anxious to get to the subject of latent interest, and did not care to discuss a point which in one and the highest sense I was agreed with the Dæmon on. "What," I asked, "was that impulse which urges me to go to the Blue Mountain? Shall I find there anything supernatural?"

"Anything supernatural? What is there above nature or outside of it?"

"But nothing is without cause; and, for an emotion so strong as I experienced on the sight of that mountain, there must have been one." I was, without knowing it, already under the control of the influence, be it delusion, be it mystery, which had possessed me, and I no longer resisted the impression of its reality. I began to feel it as a responsible being, something beyond and above me.

"Very likely! If you go after the cause you will find it! Did you expect to find some beautiful enchantress keeping her court on the mountain-top with a suite of fairies?"

I winced; for, absurd as it may seem, that very idea, half-formed, undeveloped from the latent self-ridicule involved in it, had appeared to my consciousness though I had hardly recognised it. I replied, at a loss for a reply, "And are there no such things possible?"

"All things are possible to the imagination."

"To create?"

"Most certainly! Is not creation the act of bringing into existence? and does not your Hamlet exist as immortally and really as your Shakespeare? The only true existence, is it not that of the idea? Have you not seen the pines transfigured?"

"And if I imagined a race of fairies inhabiting the Blue Mountain, should I find them?"

"If you imagined them, yes! But the imagination is not voluntary; it works to supply a necessity; its function is creation, and creation is needed only to fill a vacuum. The wild Arab, feeling his own insignificance, and comprehending the necessity of a Creating Power, finds between himself and that Power, which to him, as to you the other day, assumes a personality, an immense distance, and fills the space with an intermediate race, half-divine, half-human. It was the mental necessity for the fairy which created the fairy. You do not feel the same distance between yourself and the Creator, and so you do not call into existence a creative race of the same character— the attempts of an enlightened race to write new fairy stories, not believing in fairies, shows the incompatibility; but has not your own imagination furnished you with images to which you may give your reverence? It may be that you diminish that distance by degrading the Great First Cause to an image of your own personality, and so you are not as wise as the Arab, who at once admits it to be incomprehensible and therefore beyond his thought. Each man shapes that which he looks up to by his fears or his desires, and these in their turn are the results of his development and the measure of its degree."

"But God the Father, is He not the Great First Cause, the Supreme Creator?"

"Is it not as we said, that you measure the Supreme by yourself? Can you not comprehend a supreme law, an order which controls all things?" This touched on a theme which I had a dread of opening to myself, having once already had an experience of scepticism which left painful memories, and I did not think a distinct reply. The Dæmon, after a pause, went on: "You seem always to depend on a form for your recognitions; is not a form the result of some action, and how can the result be the finality? Every form is the form of something; of what is your conception of Deity the form of?"

Not wishing to carry this subject further, for I felt my incompetence to completely master it, and the recurrence in this mysterious manner of the question which had forced itself on me at other times and in other ways, I shrank from this discussion, and, as the hiatus must be filled, I turned the inquiry on my interlocutor.

"Tell me," I said; "do you not take cognisance of my personality? Do you read my past and future?"

"Your past and your future are contained in your present. Who can analyse what you are, can see the things which made you such; for effect contains its cause—to see the future it needs only to know the laws which govern all things. It is a simple problem: you being given, with the inevitable tendencies to which you are subject, the result is your future; the flight of one of your rifle balls cannot be calculated with greater certainty."

"But how shall we learn those laws?" I asked.

"You contain them all, for you are the result of them; and they are always the same, not one for your beginning and another for your continuance. Man is the complete embodiment of all the laws thus far developed, and you have only to know yourself to know the history of creation."

This I could not deny to be true in one sense; but, wearied and perplexed, I declined to ask anything further. I returned to camp and went to sleep. Several days passed without any progress in my knowledge of this strange influence, or what it might be, though I was more constantly sensible to its pressure every day; and, at the same time, the incomprehensible sympathy with nature, for I know not what else to call it, seemed growing stronger as the time went on and more startling in the effects it produced on the landscape. The influence was no longer confined to twilight, but made noonday mystical; and I began to hear strange sounds and words spoken by disembodied voices, as had once before happened at the beginning, but now continually. They were not accompanied by that feeling of a personal presence as when the Dæmon was present. It seemed as if the vibrations in the air shaped themselves into words, some of them of the strangest and most unexpected significance. I heard my name called, and on one occasion actually crossed the lake to ferry over what I supposed to be a friend come to see me; and heard wild laughing at night. I asked the Dæmon what it meant, and only received a guarded answer, "You would be wiser not knowing too much."

Ere many days of this solitary life had passed, alone mentally, for with Steve I never conversed but of the material want of our condition, I found my whole existence taken up with these fantasies. I determined to make my excursion to the Blue Mountain; and sending Steve down to the post-office, a three days' trip, I took my boat, with Carlo and my rifle and two days' food, and pushed off. The outlet of the Blue Mountain lakes, like those of all the Adirondack lakes, is narrow, dark, and shut in by forest, which scarcely permits landing anywhere. Now and then a log fallen into the stream compels the voyager to get out and lift his boat over; then a shallow rapid must be dragged over; and when the stream is clear of obstructions, it is too narrow for any mode of propulsion but poling or paddling. I worked along in these various ways till long past midday, and then I came out on a wide stretch of marshy land, through which the stream filtered with scarcely a visible or navigable channel, and beyond which lay the lake, and beyond the lake the Blue Mountain, the foreground being occupied with fir scrub a few feet high, and partly shutting out of view the lake itself, along the shore of which was the usual line of forest trees, amongst them occasional tall white pines, like those which had at first bewildered me. Of these, two stood at the exit of the stream from the lake, and already the weird feeling of the earlier days seized me. They seemed to forbid my entrance. I drew up my boat on the boggy shore and climbed into the tallest tamarack that grew there, high enough to look over the low wood and see the farther shore of the lake itself.

Never shall I forget what I saw from that swaying lookout. Before me was the mountain, clothed in forest to within a few hundred feet from the summit, which showed bare rock with firs clinging in the clefts and on the tables, and which was crowned by what seemed to me a walled city, the parapets of whose walls cut with a sharp, straight line against the sky, and beyond showed spire and turret and the tops of tall trees. The walls must have been, to my measuring, at least a hundred feet high, gauged by the trees, and I could see here and there between the groups of firs traces of a road coming down the mountain side. In a saner moment, I should have seen that this was only the accident of the formation, but then it kindled me like inspiration. And then I heard one of those mocking voices in the air say, "The city of Silence," as one had before said, "The procession of the Anakim." It seemed at the moment that I had only to launch through the air to reach the city, and why I did not attempt it I could hardly say. My blood rushed through my veins with a mad energy, and my brain seemed to have been replaced by some ethereal substance and to be capable of floating me off as if it were a balloon. Yet I clung and looked, my whole soul in my eyes, and had no thought of losing the spectacle even for an instant, were it to reach the city itself. The glorious glamour of that place and moment, who can comprehend it? The wind swung my tree-top to and fro, and I climbed up it until the tree bent with my weight like a twig with a bird's.

Presently I heard bells and strains of music, as though all the military bands of a large city were coming together on the walls; and the sounds rose and fell with the wind—one moment entirely lost, another full and triumphant. Then I heard the sound of hunting horns and the baying of a pack of hounds, deep-mouthed, as if a hunting party were coming down the mountain-side. Nearer and nearer they came, and I heard merry laughing and shouting as they swept through the valley, and I had a horrible dread lest they should find me and drive me, intruding, from the enchanted land.

The agitation grew so that I determined, *coute qui coute*, to fathom the mystery. I descended to the ground and pushed my way through to the lake. Near the guardian pines they lost their menace; and when I had, after long and hard work, launched my boat on the waters, I found no mystery—the mountain-top before me was a common-place mountain-top, and all the enchantment had withdrawn again. There was a fever in my blood, and a fainting weakness took the place of the mad enthusiasm of an hour before. I felt that to return to Raquette Lake was beyond my powers, and to pass the night there was nothing but to sleep under my overturned boat on the fir branches. With Carlo to keep guard, I knew that I was in no danger from the wolves, and I had food enough for him and me. I looked about the lake to find the most promising place for a sleeping-place, with a water-source; and, while I watched, I caught sight of a thin column of smoke rising from the trees at the farther end of the sheet of water.

Sick from the reaction of my delusions, inwardly ashamed of them and of myself, I paddled slowly down to the place whence the smoke arose. I found there a camp, deserted for the moment; and, drawing the boat up on the shore, I sat down on the bed of branches in the camp to await the return of the owner and ask for a night's lodging. I was weak, and, trembling from the reaction, for the eager quest of the morning was dead, I fell asleep, and woke at the growl of Carlo, announcing an approaching footstep. The owner of the camp was not far away, and welcomed me in his rough cordiality, with few words, to share his lodgings. He was a trapper engaged in running his lines for the next winter's sable trapping. He cut some venison steaks and I produced some bread, which he had not eaten for days, and we, having eaten heartily, lay down and slept till daylight. How dull and grey the landscape was in the morning twilight! My host, willing to take the opportunity to go down to Wilbur's on Raquette Lake for supplies, accepted my invitation to a seat in my boat and give me the aid of his stronger arm to work our way back. The dull and matter-of-fact life of the next day or two was beyond my power to lighten by any effort or labour, and it was not till three or four days had passed that I cared to approach my Dæmon. To my question as to the meaning of my experience of a few days before, it replied, "It was a freak of your imagination."

"But what is this imagination, then?" I asked, "which, being a faculty of my own, yet masters my reason?"

"Not at all a faculty, but your very highest self, your own life in an activity, perhaps abnormal, or even morbid, but always your own life in creative function. Your reason is a faculty, and is always subject to the purposes of your imagination. If, instead of regarding imagination as an appendage to your mental organisation, you had conceived it as it is, the highest state of your whole being, your life in its noblest function, you would have seen why it is that it works unconsciously, just as you live unconsciously and involuntarily. Men set their reason and feeling to subdue what they consider a treacherous element in themselves; they only succeed in dwarfing their natures and materialising and stifling their best selves, and succeed in keeping imagination inert while reason has the control; but when reason rests in sleep and you cease to live to the material world, imagination resumes its normal power. You dream; it is only the revival or imperfect issue of the creation you suppress when awake. You consider the sights and sounds of your late experience to be follies; you reason—imagination demonstrates its power by overturning your reason and deceiving your very senses. The madman, in whom reason has gone definitely to sleep, has nothing left him but his imagination and the habits of his appetites; but his imagination has only lost the guide to its evolution, which is all that your reason is."

"You speak of its creations," I replied. "I understand this in a certain sense; but, if these were such, would they not insist on permanence? and can anything created perish?"

"Nonsense! what will these trees be to-morrow? and the rocks you are sitting on, are they not changing to vegetation under you? The only creation is that of ideas; things are thin shadows. If man is not imaginative—*i.e.*, creative—he is still undeveloped."

"But is not such an assumption trenching on the supremacy of God?" I asked.

"What do you understand by 'God,' and where do you place Him?"

"An infinitely wise and loving Controller of events, of course," I said. "I do not attempt to define Him, but I recognise Him."

"Did you ever find anyone whose ideas of God were the same as your own?" it asked.

"Not entirely."

"Then your God is not the same as the God of other men; from the Feejeean to the Christian there is a wide range. Of course, there is a first great principle of life; but this personality you all worship—is it not a creation of your own?"

I now felt this to be the ultimate end of the Dæmon's urging: it recurred too often not to be designed. Led on by the sophistry of the Tempter, I had floated on unconsciously to this issue, practically admitting, and half-believing all; but when this suggestion stood completely unclothed before me, everything in me revolted from the abyss it opened. For an instant all was chaos, and the very order of nature seemed disorder. Life and light vanished from the face of the earth; my night made all things dead and dark. An universe without a God! Creation seemed in that moment but a galvanised corpse. What my emotions were in that brief space no one who has not felt them can conceive. My first impulse was to finish with all questionings in death; with the next I was swept back to the old life of unhesitating faith and daily reverence for the Creator, and I cried from the depth of despair, "God deliver me from the body of this death!" It was but a moment—and then there came in the place of the cold questioning voice of the Daemon one of ineffable music, repeating words familiar from my childhood and lovely in my past, "Ye believe in God—believe also in me." The hot tears for another moment blotted out the world from sight. I said passionately to the questioner, "Now, who are you? what are you?" "Your own doubts," was the reply, and it was as if I spoke to myself. Little by little I grew clearer, and after the state had long gone by, it seemed as if I had been in a long and troubled dream. But the experience never came back—the lesson was learned.

THE PHILOSOPHERS' CAMP

I REMEMBER that in one of his early letters to me, Professor Ruskin expressed the opinion that the character of American landscape was such as not to favour invention, but that its largeness must give the art a high degree of grandeur, once excited. It was true, for the sameness of the wild nature is not much relieved by the incomplete domestication, where men have improved its humanisation — it lacks the appeals to human sympathy and imagination which are made by the landscape of an old country, and what Theodore Rousseau used to call *intimité*, which is partially interpreted by our feeling of association — the presence of a "light that never was on sea or land." I have always found that it lacked the quality of the pictorial, which is so abounding in English and Italian scenery and some parts of the lands of France, and the search for the picturesque was one of the great pre-occupations of the landscape painter when I was a student. In default of a motive in the familiar scenes, we used to frequent the wild ones, and the great, untracked wildernesses of the Northern states were a field of study and search of emotion — the sentiment of savage nature, since the picturesque was not at our doors. The huge forest of the

Adirondack region of New York state, threaded by rivers, and interspersed with lakes of all sizes from Champlain, where fleets once fought, to the tiny sheets of water where the skiff passes with difficulty through the fields of pond-lilies, was that which most caught my imagination; and for several years I passed the summer there, more fascinated by the solitude and savagery of it than by anything paintable I found there. The relations with Lowell and the University town of Cambridge, alluded to in another paper, led him and some of his friends to share the fortunes of one of my excursions, recorded in "The Subjective of It," and from this to the formation of a club, known as the Adirondack, amongst whose members were Lowell, Emerson, Agassiz, Professor Jeffries Wyman (the rare scientific genius taken from his studies too soon for the honour of his country), Dr Estes Howe, Judge Hoar (General Grant's Attorney-General later on), S. G. Ward, J. M. Forbes, and others amongst the leading personages of Boston and Cambridge. The club existed until the war absorbed all the thought of its members, and the estate of over 20,000 acres of untouched and primitive forest in the wildest and most beautiful part of the Adirondacks was allowed to be re-conveyed to the lumber cutters.

But the first meeting was of unique interest, from its having given rise to incidents and records which survived the duration of the club. Chief amongst these is the poem in which Emerson recorded his impressions of the first contact with primeval nature. The excursion also brought the section into an unenviable notoriety, and so set the fashion of luxurious camping out, and purchase of tracts of land in the forest, which have, in the sequence, destroyed its original character altogether. Then the wolf howled and the bear prowled about our camps, and more than once have I heard the cry of the panther (*Felis puma*) as it skirted our vicinity; the grey eagle was almost the commonest of birds, and one might pass a fortnight in the forest without seeing another human being. The estate, which we afterwards purchased at tax sale, included a pretty lake a mile and a half long, with islands, all untouched still by the lumberer's axe, the forest standing as it had stood before Columbus sailed from Palos; and the larger lake where we made our initiatory meeting, though of easier access, was in the same condition. The condition of the club meeting was, that for six weeks the camp should be open to all the members and guests invited by the committee, after or before which members were free to invite their friends and occupy the camp without restriction, each person having his own guide and boat and exploring the forest around or remaining in camp at pleasure, forming parties or moving independently, lapsing as far as might be into the original state of society.

The mountain country, which is known collectively as the "Adirondack," is an elevated plateau of the Laurentian range, lying between the valleys of the Mohawk and St Lawrence, deeply cut by vales and gorges amongst the granite hills, and in every depression holding a lake, the water connection of which, with its companions, gives rise to the characteristic feature of the region, each chain of lakes forming a water-course, through which lie the routes which explore the entire region, it being rarely the case that more than a mile separates the water of one chain from that of another. The guides use light boats, which they can easily carry on their shoulders from one water to the next, and so they traverse the entire mountain country freely. The lake where our first encampment was made was known as Follansbee Pond (the term lake being, in the section, reserved for a sheet of several miles in length), and it lies in a *cul-de-sac* of the chain of lakes and streams named after one of the first of the Jesuit explorers of the northern states, Pere Raquette. Being elected captain of the hunt and chief guide of the club, it depended on me also, as the oldest woodsman, to select the locality and superintend the construction of the camp, and the choice was determined by the facility of access, the abundance of game, and the fact that the lake was out of any route to regions beyond, giving the maximum of seclusion, as the etiquette of the woods prevented another party camping near us.

Follansbee was then a rare and beautiful piece of untouched nature, divided from the highway, the Raquette, by a marsh of several miles of weary navigation, shut in by the hills on all sides but that by which we entered, the forest still unscarred, and the tall white pines standing in files along the lake shores and up over the ridges, not a scar of axe or fire being visible as we searched the shore for a fitting spot to make our vacation lodging-place. Many things are requisite for a good camping-ground, and to fix one is a thing to be learned. First and indispensable is a spring of good water near by; then a dry and elevated plateau, wooded with "hard wood,"— beeches, birch, and maple—with level ground for the camp, free from the tangle of undergrowth which makes the fir thicket impenetrable; then a smooth sandy beach on which the boats may be drawn at night, and which may be approached without danger from the rocks, and on which loading or unloading is easy. Ours was one of the best I have ever seen—at the head of the lake, with beach, spring, and maple grove. Two of the hugest maples I ever saw gave us the shelter of their spreading branches and the supports to the camp walls. Here we placed our ridge-pole, laid our roof of bark of firs (stripped from trees far away in the forest, not to disfigure our dwelling-place with stripped and dying trees), cut an open path to the lake-side, and then left our house to the naïads and dryads, and hurried back forty miles to meet our guests at Martin's Landing.

A generation has gone by since that unique meet, and of those who were at it only John Holmes (a younger brother of Oliver Wendell) and I now survive. The voices of that merry assemblage of "wise and polite" vacation-keepers come to us from the land of dreams; the echoes they wakened in the wild wood give place to the tender and tearful evocation of poetic memory; they and their summering have passed into the traditions of the later camp-fires, where the guides tell of the "Philosophers' Camp," of the very location of which they have lost the knowledge. But Emerson, the philosopher whose genius was fittest to the temple in which we all worshipped, its high priest and oracle, has left his history of the meeting in his poem, "The Adirondacs. A Journal. Dedicated to my fellow-travellers in August, 1858," and to which my prose may serve as commentary, to be written before I have done with the memory. I, the youngest, the steward of that memorable company, the master of the hunt, the insect preserved in the amber of the poet's verse,

"Our guide's guide, and Commodore,
Crusoe, Crusader, Pius Æneas,"

purpose to frame, even if in a poor way, this picture of a gathering unique in the history of vacations; this record, which is to those who know and love unsophisticated nature the most curiously truthful and interesting existing revelation of her aspect, seen for the first time with a mind trained to the finest shades of impression and reflection—the most Homeric and Hellenic of all nature-poems ever written.

This was not the solitude of Thoreau's Walden Pond, where isolation kept within the sound of a dinner-horn, and where no bird, leaf, or tree was ignorant of the daily footfall of idlers and curious, but a virgin forest, where the crack of our rifles reached no other human ear, and where the carelessly wandering foot found no path to lead it back to camp, and the inexpert, once out of hearing of camp-call, or out of sight of the water, was in imminent danger of having his bones picked by the wolves that listened dismayed to the sounds of our unaccustomed invasion. This was "the forest primeval." Hardly a trace of it now exists as we then knew it. The lumberer; the reckless sportsman with his camp-fires and his more reckless and careless guide; the axe and the fire, have left no large expanse of virgin forest in all the Adirondack region, and every year effaces the original aspect of it more completely. Then there were no song-birds, companions of mankind; no familiar sound of the paternal fields greeted the wise men of the East: but the weird laugh of the loon, the scream of the osprey or the grey eagle; and of the minor featherlings, the friendly Canada jay or the chickadee, only greeted us.

I had done all I could to induce Longfellow and Oliver Wendell Holmes to join the party, but the latter was too closely identified with the Hub in all his mental operations to care for unhumanised nature, and Longfellow was too strongly attached to the conditions of completely civilised life to enjoy roughing it in flannels and sleeping on fir boughs. The company of his great-brained friends was a temptation at times, I think; but he hated killing animals, had no interest in fishing, and was too settled in his habits to enjoy so great a change. Possibly he was decided in his refusal by Emerson's purchase of a rifle. "Is it true that Emerson is going to take a gun?" he asked me. "Yes," I replied. "Then I shall not go," he said; "somebody will be shot."

Emerson's record plunges *in medias res*. He gives a line to Champlain:

> "Thence, in strong country cart, rode up the forks
> Of the Ausable stream, intent to reach
> The Adirondac lakes. At Martin's Beach
> We chose our boats, each man a boat and guide,
> Ten men, ten guides, our company all told."

But here I must correct my evangelist. I was Agassiz's guide and rowed my own boat, sharing with the guides whatever work there was for all. I could not have kept in proper subordination so large a company of men, collected from all parts of the woods, though with all the care in selection possible under the circumstances, if I had not been ready to do my share of any work I called on them for. I not only rowed my own boat, but carried my own axe and rifle, and my boat when necessary. From one cause I missed, to my infinite regret, the hearing of Emerson's first impressions of the forest. I had been building a new boat for the occasion, and it lacked several hours' work when the company started up the lakes at midday, I only following toward sunset, and overtaking them at midnight at the "Indian Carry," then a mere

THE PHILOSOPHERS' CAMP

pathway a mile long, through dense pine groves, between the Saranac and Raquette chains of lakes, with a lumberer's hut at each end. A violent rainstorm greeted our entry into the wilderness, and I arrived after the company were dried and had eaten, myself drenched like a water-rat.

Emerson wrote out his "Adirondacs" after he had returned to Concord, and it is curious to see in what a Greek way he condensed and idealised his impressions, forgetting all details which interfered with symmetry.

> "Next morn we swept with oars the Saranac,
> With skies of benediction, to Round Lake,
> Where all the sacred mountains drew around us,
> Taháwus, Seaward,* MacIntyre, Baldhead,
> And other Titans without muse or name.
> Pleased with these grand companions, we glide on,
> Instead of flowers, crowned with a wreath of hills.
> We made our distance wider, boat from boat,
> As each would hear the oracle alone.
> By the bright morn the gay flotilla slid
> Through files of flags that gleamed like bayonets,
> Through gold-moth-haunted beds of pickerel-flower,
> Through scented banks of lilies white and gold,
> Where the deer feeds at night, the teal by day.
> On through the Upper Saranac, and up
> Père Raquette stream, to a small tortuous pass
> Winding through grassy shallows in and out,
> Two creeping miles of rushes, pads, and sponge,
> To Follansbee Water and the Lake of Loons."

The poet has painted his picture with the grouping of an artist's imagination. The drenching day of arrival, the night of discomfort at the hut on the "carry," and the "carry" itself, the journey

* Mount Seward, south of the Saranacs, the common name being repudiated by Emerson.

through the "Spectacle Ponds," a curious and most picturesque part of the second day, with the row down the charming stream that forms the waterway to the Raquette proper—all are dismissed as useless detail, while the "two creeping miles" of the marshy outlet of Follansbee, up which we had to pole and push, are remembered through Agassiz's discovery there of a fresh-water sponge till then unknown. But to Emerson, as to most men who are receptive to nature's message, the forest was the overpowering fact.

> "We climb the bank,
> And in the twilight of the forest noon
> Wield the first axe these echoes ever heard."

The "twilight of the forest noon" is the most concentrated expression of the one dominant sentiment of a poetic mind on first entering this eternal silence and shadow. His catalogue of trees is in error:

> "The wood was sovran with centennial trees—
> Oak, cedar, maple, poplar, beech, and fir,
> Linden and spruce."

There is no oak, linden, or poplar in these forests. He had passed them in the Ausable valley on his way up, and probably forgot their exact habitat. But the impression of the first night clung to him with all its detail. No modern man knew the "great god Pan" as Emerson knew him,—not even Keats, —and the falling asleep in the arms of the universal mother, whose dearest child Pan was, must have left its influence on him long after he had recorded the poetic version of the experience.

"'Welcome!' the wood-god murmured through the leaves,—
'Welcome, though late, unknowing, yet known to me.'
Evening drew on; stars peeped through maple-boughs,
Which o'erhung, *like a cloud*,* our camping-fire.
Decayed millennial trunks, like moonlight flecks,
Lit with phosphoric crumbs† the forest floor."

Lowell named the camping-place "Camp Maple," from the huge maples under which we had pitched our house of bark; but tradition has long known it as the "Philosophers' Camp," though, like Troy, its site is unknown to all the subsequent generations of guides, and I doubt if in all the Adirondack country there is a man except my old guide, Steve Martin, who could point out the place where it stood.

To me the forest was familiar. I knew it as a boy charged with sophomorical sentiment, casting about to find what inspiration I ought to borrow from nature; and I had ploughed the field too often to find any genuine crop on it. I had passed months painting in the glades, had wandered and boated in the forest and on the streams till I felt the points of the compass in the dark, and knew its material fact as I knew my bedroom; but I had come to look on it as one does on one of those curious shells which some insects cast, and which keep the form from which the life has escaped. It was to me empty; it no longer lured me with

* This is a singularly faithful expression of the appearance of the massive foliage of those lofty trees lighted by the camp-fires beneath.

† The decayed tree-trunks, falling into ruin, often looked like glow-worms in the dark of night, their phosphorescence being frequently brilliant.

any emotion beyond that of quiet, the charm of Lethe, the fascination of an almost complete negation of intellectual existence, and absolute rest. I was therefore profoundly interested in Emerson's first impressions, and we were much together. I rowed him into the innermost recesses of Follansbee Water, and would, at his request, sometimes land him in a solitary part of the lake-shore, and leave him to his emotions or studies. We had no post, and letters neither came nor went, and so, probably, none record the moment's mood; but well I remember how he marvelled at the completeness of the circle of life in the forest. He examined the guides, and me as one of them, with the interest of a discoverer of a new race. Me he had known in another phase of existence — at the club, in the multitude, one of the atoms of the social whole. To find me axe in hand, ready for the elementary functions of a savage life—to fell the trees, to kill the deer, or catch the trout, and at need to cook them — in this to him new phenomenon of a rounded and self-sufficient individuality, waiting for, and waited on, by no one, he received a conception of life which had the same attraction in its completeness and roundness that a larger and fully organised existence would have had. It was a form of independence which he had never realised before, and he paid it the respect of a new discovery. He had become weary of the social completeness as a study, it seemed to me; it was too large and exacting. But now

THE PHILOSOPHERS' CAMP

he found a man who could be taken up as a specimen, and studied as an individual, as Agassiz would have studied a fossil; and all this was new.

Emerson, as I read him, had no self-sufficiency. He lived and felt with the minimum of personal colour, reflecting nature and man; and the study of the guide, the savage man thrown out of society like a chip from a log under the axe of the chopper, returning to the status of pure individuality — men such as our guides were — aroused in the philosopher the enthusiasm of a new fact. He often spoke of it, and watched the men as a naturalist does the animals he classifies. I remember Longfellow's once saying of Emerson that he used his friends as one did lemons—when he could squeeze nothing more from them, he threw them away; but this, while in one sense true, does Emerson a radical injustice. He had no vanity, no self-importance; truth and philosophy were so supreme in their hold on him that neither his self nor any other self was worth so much as the solution of a problem in life. To get this solution he was willing to squeeze himself like a lemon, if need were; and why should he be otherwise disposed to his neighbour? There are others who knew Emerson better than I did or could, and possibly Longfellow did, though that observation makes me doubt that there was any real sympathy between them. But what seems to me the truth is, that Emerson instinctively divided men into two classes, with one of which he formed personal attachments which, though tranquil and undemonstrative, as was his nature, were lasting; in the other he simply found his objects of study, problems to be solved and their solutions recorded. There was the least conceivable self-assertion in him; he was the best listener a genuine thinker, or one whom he thought to be such, ever had; and always seemed to prefer to listen rather than to talk, to observe and study rather than to discourse. So he did not say much before nature; he took in her influences as the earth takes the rain. He was minutely interested in seeing how the old guides reversed the tendencies of civilisation: how when they went to sleep on the ground they put on their coats, but took them off when they got up; wore their hats in camp, but went on the lake bareheaded.

The entire absorption of his personality in the subject-matter of study was childlike; he left no cranny of novelty unsearched. I remember that one Sunday morning, when the state of the larder made it necessary for the guides to get a deer, Emerson was more disposed for quiet meditation, having at that time no interest in the hunt; so I took him in my boat, and while those of the company whose habits did not interfere with the enjoyment of the chase on Sunday went to the watching-posts with the guides, we sought the remotest nook of the lake-shore. It was a magnificent morning, and in the silence of the forest the baying of the hounds, as they took the scent on the hills above us and followed

THE PHILOSOPHERS' CAMP 279

the deer in his doublings and evasions, filled the air, and the echoes redoubled the music. When the deer are in good condition, as in August, they generally take a long run before they come to water, and we heard the dogs sweeping round over the hills at the farther end of the lake, and coming back, ranging to and fro, till the expectancy and the new sensation grew in effect on Emerson, and he could resist no longer. "Let us go after the deer!" he exclaimed; and though, having come out for meditation, we had no gun with us, we were soon flying down the lake from our remotest corner to where the baying led to the shore. But we were too late; Lowell had already killed the deer before we got there.

It was interesting to see how Emerson grew into the camp life. As at first he had refused to carry a rifle, and decided to take one only for uniformity, so, in the early days of our forest residence, he declined to take any part in the hunting or fishing; but we had not been long in camp before he caught the temper of the occasion, and began to desire to kill his deer. Luck failed him in the drives in which he took part, the deer always coming in to some other watcher, and we decided to try night-hunting—*i.e.*, stealing up to the deer as they browse in the pads along the shallow water, carrying in the bow of the boat a light which blinds the animal, the lantern throwing all its light forward, and the hunter sitting invisible in the shadow. This manner of hunting is possible only on very dark nights, and was resorted to only when venison was needed and the drive had failed. If the man who paddles the boat is dexterous, the deer can be approached to within a few yards without being alarmed; but in the darkness it is very difficult for those not accustomed to the appearance of the animal to distinguish him from the rocks or shrubs around, for in the intent examination of the strange phenomenon of the light he remains motionless, except that now and then he will beat the water with his hoofs to drive away the flies. We took the best guide at the paddle, Emerson taking the firing-seat behind the lamp, and I in the middle with my rifle ready, in case he missed his shot.

We went down the lake to the large bay at the left of the outlet, now noted on the map of the State survey as "Agassiz Bay," which is a mistake, for we named this "Osprey Bay," from the osprey nest in one of its tall pines, the bay opposite the camp at the south end of the lake being named in honour of Agassiz. The shore is an alternation of stretches of sandy beach where the white pond-lily thrives, and offers food for the deer, and rocky points separate the beaches as if by screens, so that any movement in one of the little bays is not visible in another. There is something weird in silently gliding along a spectral diorama of irrecognisable landscape, with rocks and trees slipping by like phantasms; for the motion of the boat is not distinguishable, and the only sound is the occasional grating of

THE PHILOSOPHERS' CAMP

the rushes on the bottom of the boat. It is, in fact, the most exciting form of deer-hunting for certain temperaments, and the poet was strongly impressed. The practised ear of the guide soon caught the sound of the footfall of a deer making his way down to the shore, and he turned the glare of the lamp on the beach, moving directly on him till he was within twenty yards. The signal to fire was given and repeated, but Emerson could distinguish nothing. "Shoot!" finally whispered the guide in the faintest breath. "Shoot!" I repeated nearer. But the deer was invisible to him, and we drifted to a boat's length from him before the animal took fright and bolted for the woods, undisturbed by a hasty shot I sent after him, and we heard his triumphant whistle and gallop dying away in the forest depths. Emerson was stupefied. We rounded the next point, and found a deer already on the feeding-ground, to repeat the experience. The deer stood broadside to him, in full view, in the shallow water; but, straining his vision to the utmost, he could distinguish nothing like a deer, and when we had got so near that the same result was imminent, I fired, and the buck fell dead. "Well," said Emerson, "if that was a deer, I shall fire at the first square thing I see"; but we saw no more that night. He records the impression:

"Or, later yet, beneath a lighted jack,
In the boat's bows, a silent night-hunter

> Stealing with paddle to the feeding-grounds
> Of the red deer, to aim at a square mist.
> Hark to that muffled roar! A tree in the woods
> Is fallen: but hush! it has not scared the buck,
> Who stands astonished at the meteor light,
> Then turns to bound away,—is it too late?"

Each disappointment, however, plunged him more deeply into the excitement of the chase, and he was most anxious to kill his deer before he went home, unable to resist the contagion of the passion for it. He said to me one day, "I must kill a deer before we go home, even if the guide has to hold him by the tail." At that season of the year, when the deer are in their "short coat," the body sinks at once if shot in the deep water; and on overtaking the quarry in the lake, if the deer-slayer was not sure of his shot, the guide used to run the boat alongside of it, and catch it by the tail, when the shot became a sure one. As we hunted only when we needed the meat, we did not risk the loss of the deer, and when a poor shot held the gun, the quarry was caught by the tail and killed in this unsportsmanlike way. That survival of the earliest passion of the primitive man, the passion of the chase, overcame even the philosophic mind of Emerson, once exposed to the original influences, and he recognised his ancestral bent. Few of us who live an active life fail to be attracted by this first of all occupations of the yet uncivilised man. Emerson never had the gratification of his desire; the deer never came to him on the drive, and his repetition of the night-hunt was no more successful.

The starry magnificence of those nights, with their pure mountain air, was another source of delight hardly to be imagined by those who have not known it by experience. There seemed to be more stars visible than anywhere else I had ever been, and we were often out on the lake till near midnight;

> "Or, in the evening twilight's latest red,
> Beholding the procession of the pines,"—

a curious phenomenon, now, with the ravages of fire and axe, become a thing of the past. The tall white pines, which when full grown rise from one hundred and fifty to two hundred feet, towering nearly half their height above the mass of deciduous trees, and beyond the protection which the solid forest gives against the dominant west winds, acquire a leaning to the east; and as they grew in long lines along the shores, or followed the rocky ridges up the mountain sides, they seemed to be gigantic human beings moving in procession to the east. I had the year before painted a picture of the subject, and Emerson had been struck by it at the Athenæum exhibition; and when we were established in camp, almost the first thing he asked to see was the "procession of the pines"; and our last evening on the lake was spent together watching the glow dying out behind a noble line of the marching pines on the shore of Follansbee Water.

In memory of that summer, and the intimacy of camp life which strips the man of all disguises, Emerson seems to me to be magnified with the lapse of time, as Mont Blanc towers above his fellows with distance. For Lowell, I had a passionate personal attachment to which death and time have only given a twilight glory; for Agassiz, I had the feeling which all had who came under the magic of his colossal individuality—the myriad-minded one to whom nothing came amiss or unfamiliar, and who had a facet for every man he came in contact with. His inexhaustible *bonhomie* won even the guides to a personal fealty they showed no other of our band; his wide science gave us continual lectures on all the elements of nature — no plant, no insect, no quadruped hiding its secret from him. The lessons he taught us of the leaves of the pine, and of the vicissitudes of the Laurentian range, in one of whose hollows we lay; the way he drew new facts from the lake, and knew them when he saw them, as though he had set his seal on them before they were known; the daily dissection of the fish, the deer, the mice (for which he had brought his traps), were studies in which we were his assistants and pupils. All this made being with him not only "a liberal education," but perpetual sunshine and good fortune. When we went out, I at the oars and he at the dredge or insect-net, or examining the plants by the marsh-side, his spirit was a perpetual spring of science. When he and Wyman entered on the discussion of a scientific subject (and they always worked together), science seemed as easy as versification when

Lowell was in the mood, and all sat around inhaling wisdom with the mountain air. Nothing could have been, to any man with the scientific bent, more intensely interesting than the academy of two of the greatest scientists of their day. Wyman's was a gentle, womanlike nature, modest to a fault, utterly absorbed in his science, and free from a shadow of pretension. He was held by many to be the greater scientist, but the personality of Agassiz towered over every other about him, and won all suffrages for the day. But looking back across the gulf which hides all the details of life, the eternal absence which forgets personal qualities, the calm, platonic serenity of Emerson stands out from all our company as a crystallisation of impersonal and universal humanity; no vexation, no mishap could disturb his philosophy, or rob him of its lesson.

At our dinners, the semblance of which life will never offer me again, the gods sent their best accompaniments and influences—health, appetite, wit, and poetry, with good digestion.

> "Our foaming ale we drank from hunters' pans—
> Ale, and a sup of wine. Our steward gave
> Venison and trout, potatoes, beans, wheat-bread.
> All ate like abbots, and, if any missed
> Their wonted convenience, cheerly hid the loss
> With hunter's appetite and peals of mirth."

Lowell was the Magnus Apollo of the camp. His Castalian humour, his unceasing play of wit and erudition—poetry and the best of the poets always on tap at the table—all know them who knew him well, though not many as I did; but when he sat on one side of the table, and Judge Hoar (the most pyrotechnical wit I have ever known) and he were matching table-talk, with Emerson and Agassiz to sit as umpires and revive the vein as it menaced to flag, Holmes and Estes Howe not silent in the well-matched contest, the forest echoed with such laughter as no club ever knew, and the owls came in the trees overhead to wonder. These were symposia to which fortune has invited few men, and which no one invited could ever forget.

The magical quality of the forest is that of oblivion of all that is left in the busy world—of past trouble and coming care. The steeds that brought us in had no place behind for black care. We lived, as Emerson says,

> "Lords of this realm,
> Bounded by dawn and sunset, and the day
> Rounded by hours where each outdid the last
> In miracles of pomp, we must be proud,
> As if associates of the sylvan gods.
> We seemed the dwellers of the zodiac,
> So pure the Alpine element we breathed,
> So light, so lofty pictures came and went."

At sunrise, the guides and we who had cares of the camp were afoot; fires were refreshed, bathers went out, and a boat went to look at the set lines for trout. Breakfast was at eight. Then we practised firing at a mark, a few rounds each, the scientists dissected their specimens, and

THE PHILOSOPHERS' CAMP

the guides did the "house-work." I made a study as the memorial of the event—the morning hour in the camp: Agassiz and Wyman on one side dissecting a trout, with the assistance of Howe and Holmes; on the other, the firing party, Lowell, Judge Hoar, and the rest of us, except Emerson, who professed to be neither rifleman nor anatomist, but with a pilgrim's staff in hand took a place alone and between the two groups, with an intentional symbolism of his position in the world. Then, if venison was wanted, we set the hunt; or those who chose to wander did so, explored the streams and woods around, botanised, hunted specimens, or fished.

> "Ask you, how went the hours?
> All day we swept the lake, searched every cove,
> North from Camp Maple, south to Osprey Bay,
> Watching when the loud dogs should drive in deer,
> Or whipping its rough surface for a trout;
> Or, bathers, diving from the rock at noon;
> Challenging Echo by our guns and cries;
> Or listening to the laughter of the loon.
> . . . .
> Our heroes tried their rifles at a mark,
> Six rods, sixteen, twenty, or forty-five;
> Sometimes their wits at sally and retort,
> With laughter sudden as the crack of rifle;
> Or parties scaled the near acclivities,
> Competing seekers of a rumoured lake,
> Whose unauthenticated waves we named
> Lake Probability,—our carbuncle,
> Long sought, not found.
>
> Two doctors in the camp
> Dissected the slain deer, weighed the trout's brain,
> Captured the lizard, salamander, shrew,

> Crab, mice, snail, dragon-fly, minnow, and moth;
> Insatiate skill in water or in air
> Waved the scoop-net, and nothing came amiss;
> The while, one leaden pot of alcohol
> Gave an impartial tomb to all the kinds.
> Not less the ambitious botanist sought plants—
> Orchis and gentian, fern and long whip-scirpus,
> Rosy polygonum, lake-margin's pride,
> Hypnum and hydnum, mushroom, sponge, and moss,
> Or harebell nodding in the gorge of falls."

A pleasant life it was; there was no prevention of debtor or creditor, no due-bills or trouble of business; all had put affairs by for a certain time, and day by day the Lethean silence lured us deeper into its magic recesses. The outside world was but a dream. No visitor intruded on our presence. We ate a deer every day, and the venison was such as no king ever tasted, and our lake furnished trout in perfection. The larder was always provided: not often was the drive without its deer, and if by chance two were killed in one day, we killed none the next, for we tolerated no waste or wanton killing, and the osprey, the eagle, and the loon had in us friends. The effect of this life alike on the physical and mental condition was such as only experience can estimate. It was wonderful to see how the healing of the mighty mother cured the ailments we brought with us. It was nothing new to me, but to the newcomers it was like enchantment. Agassiz came suffering from rheumatism and overwork, but four days sufficed to restore him to his normal condition. The dust that the turmoil of civilisation throws into the mental mechanism was no longer allowed to wear or weary; life and all its problems came out in a much less complex light, and the conditions of existence seemed simplified. Why should men be anxious for more, when with little we fared so well, or were so easily provided? No complication of this problem was forced on the mind, which was left in this so facile solution of it that it seemed to clear the future of all its difficulties. We seemed to have got back into a not too greatly-changed Eden, whose imperious ties to the outer world were hidden for the day in the waters and woods that lay between us and it. We had at last come to the state where what each man was and had made of himself was the real measure of his relation to the world, and the universal mother took us all on the same terms, the worst prodigal reckoned as good as he who had endured guiltlessly his temptation, the worst violator of her laws with the least sinner.

> " So fast will Nature acclimate her sons,
> Though late returning to her pristine ways.
> Off soundings, seamen do not suffer cold;
> And in the forest, delicate clerks, unbrowned,
> Sleep on the fragrant brush, as on down-beds.
> Up with the dawn, they fancied the light air
> That circled freshly in their forest dress
> Made them to boys again. Happier that they
> Slipped off their pack of duties, leagues behind,
> At the first mounting of the giant stairs.
> No placard on these rocks warned to the polls,
> No door-bell heralded a visitor,

T

> No courier waits, no letter came or went,
> Nothing was ploughed, or reaped, or bought, or sold.
> The frost might glitter, it would blight no crop;
> The falling rain would spoil no holiday.
> We were made freemen of the forest laws,
> All dressed, like nature, fit for her own ends,
> Essaying nothing she cannot perform."

I have quoted enough to show how fully Emerson caught, in his first experience, the spirit of the woods: not morbidly, like Shelley, nor with the air of calling all the world to see how solitary he was, which seems to me so much to impair the genuineness of Thoreau's experience in the barn-door backwoods in which he acted the recluse. Thoreau was a modern realist with a morose and uncompanionable genius always in attendance; his was a pinchbeck royalty with a lunch-basket from his father's farm hardly hidden behind his throne. He saw minutely, as all short-sighted people do; Emerson, in his single interview with a true and uncontaminated nature, saw all the relations between her and not merely one individuality, narrow or large, but all humanity. The ancient Greek in him found the algebraic formula of existence, the absolute ideal of man and the law of his relation to nature. He saw "hypnum and hydnum," but put them down as details in a foreground. What filled his canvas was manhood. He measured and specialised nature with reference to a completed and ideal type in which nature was fulfilled, and he bowed to the backwoodsman.

> "Your rank is all reversed. Let men of cloth
> Bow to the stalwart churls in overalls:
> *They* are the doctors of the wilderness,
> And we the low-prized laymen."

If the experience was unique, it was sufficient, and other summers had been only repetitions; his epic of the wilderness may be made more picturesque by another telling, but not more complete. What he did in this poem is unique as was the occasion. He reduced man to his most simple condition before nature in her most primitive state and drew them as a whole, as the great painters did their outdoor figure-subjects —humanity always the keynote of the picture. When he has told nature's message, he gives by implication something beyond the interpretation of it as rendered in thought, the recognition of what it does with humanity. Taking man in the simple and complete type, to which he does full honour, as he reverences nature; beyond this and that there stands always the higher and ultimate universal nature of which man is a part, but the crowning part, the aspiring and suffering humanity. There is no conflict; only, when all has been said for the backwoods and the backwoodsman, he points to another humanity and nature beyond.

> "And presently the sky is changed; O world!
> What pictures and what harmonies are thine!
> The clouds are rich and dark, the air serene,
> *So like the soul of me, what if 'twere me?*
> A melancholy better than all mirth.

> Comes the sweet sadness at the retrospect,
> Or at the foresight of obscurer years?
>
> . . . .
>
> And, that no day of life may lack romance,
> The spiritual stars rise nightly, shedding down
> A private beam into each several heart.
>
> . . . .
>
> Suns haste to set, that so remoter lights
> Beckon the wanderer to his vaster home."

In the midst of this hymn to nature, it was one of the supreme achievements of the mechanical mind of man which furnished the text for his loudest pæan. Some of the members of the company, in their wanderings outside our realm, had met a traveller with the news of the laying of the first transatlantic cable, and came back to camp with the great news.

> " One held a printed journal, waving high,
> Caught from a late-arriving traveller,
> Big with great news, and shouted the report
> For which the world had waited, now firm fact,
> Of the wire-cable laid beneath the sea,
> And landed on our coast, and pulsating
> With ductile fire. Loud, exulting cries
> From boat to boat, and to the echoes round,
> Greet the glad miracle."

Emerson is, we say, cold. Perhaps in the day when only bacchanals heat the public ear he may be so. There is no passion which the public now generally recognise as such, except the personal; but in that serener sphere where Plato breathed, the nature of Emerson is too much at home to be yet widely understood in its passion. How Greek is this passionate outburst at the new revolt of the human mind against its limitations,

THE PHILOSOPHERS' CAMP

this clapping of hands at the Promethean unloosing! And Promethean passion was his: it quickened his blood with every human footstep upward, it kindled the light of his calm eyes anew with every indignity offered humanity; not only the slavery of the black and the barbarian made his anger burn, but the slavery of civilisation and self-imposed wrong made his soul heavy.

And people have the idea of comparing him with the burly Carlyle! As well Apollo with a jotun! "Deficient in form and polish?" Well, the ages had not yet furnished the material to cut this diamond to its faceted formality; there is neither the form of Sophocles nor the fluency of Plato, but it was further from Homer to Plato than from Chaucer to Emerson. Then see the Greek again in his instinctive impersonation of the forces of nature—"Chronos and Tellus who were before Jove":

> "A spasm throbbing through the pedestals
> Of Alp and Andes, isle and continent,
> Urging astonished Chaos with a thrill
> To be a brain, or serve the brain of man.
> The lightning has run masterless too long;
> He must to school and learn his verb and noun,
> And teach his nimbleness to earn his wage,
> Spelling with guided tongue man's messages
> Shot through the weltering pit of the salt sea."

But our paradise was no Eden. The world that played bo-peep with us across the mountains came for us when the play-spell was over; this summer dream, unique in the record of poesy, melted like a cloud-castle into its original elements, and Emerson was one of the first to turn back to the sterner use of time.

> "The holidays were fruitful, but must end;
> One August evening had a cooler breath;
> Into each mind intruding duties crept;
> Under the cinders burned the fires of home;
> Nay, letters found us in our paradise:
> So in the gladness of the new event
> We struck our camp and left the happy hills."

The lake became for a time a place of pilgrimage. To visit the Philosophers' Camp was one of the items of an Adirondack trip.

> "We planned
> That we should build, hard by, a spacious lodge,
> And how we should come hither with our sons
> Hereafter."

And the permanent meeting-place was fixed at Ampersand Pond, to which in time the tradition of the Philosophers' Camp was attached, and where, as long as the club existed, the annual meetings were held.

Twenty-five years elapsed before I returned to Follansbee Water. The *genius loci*, dryad or hamadryad, had there been one, would have found it as hard to recognise me as I found it hard to find Camp Maple. I had the same guide, Steve Martin, a grey-headed man, the worse for a life of hardship, which, I find, does not always harden; but we found with great difficulty the landing and the choked-up spring. A half-reforested clearing spread round the spot where our "ten scholars" used to lie, and a tangled thicket of raspberry bushes, lady's-willow, birch saplings, and tall grass, made walking almost impossible. We found a huge rock that had been a landmark, but this and the spring alone were to be distinguished. The careless sportsmen had cut all the hard wood away, and let the fires in, and the whole forest round had been burned, and was succeeded by thickets of undergrowth. The great maples and the tall white pines had gone from the entire vicinity, and a vulgar new forest was on its way; the trees that used to line the lake-shore had fallen into the lake, their roots being burned away; and not the slightest feature remained of the grove where wit and wisdom held tournament a generation before. All was ashes and ruin. I

> "felt like one who treads alone
> Some banquet-hall deserted."

Nor was the lake less changed in outward appearance. Every fit camping-ground on the shore had been occupied in succession, and the camp-fires allowed to spread into the forest until the whole shore had been denuded of its fringe of hoary trees. The "procession of the pines" had gone by for ever; only here and there a dead trunk was standing, among them that up which Lowell's guide climbed to the osprey's nest to get an egg for Agassiz. Speculating manufacturers had built a dam across the Raquette and flooded all the bottom-land, killing the trees over a large tract; wretched dolts had put pike into the

Raquette waters, and the trout had become exterminated in every stream to which the ravenous fish had access.

It was well that the charm once broken, the desecration begun, it should be complete. The memories sacred to the few survivors can never be quickened by this ruin, and to the rest of the world it does not matter. Emerson has embalmed it; that is enough. In some Eastern countries it is the custom to break the bowl from which an honoured guest has drunk; nature has done this service to Follansbee Water.

www.ingramcontent.com/pod-product-compliance
Lightning Source LLC
Chambersburg PA
CBHW030816230426
43667CB00008B/1238